LIVING LIFE WITH
PASSION
AND HELPING OTHERS

Mike—

It was an honor getting to know you and wish you all the success in changing our world!

Carey Smolensky

CAREY SMOLENSKY

To my wife, Diane, who has been my partner in life and business for almost three decades.

To my children, Blake and Rachel, and my son-in-law Joe, I wish you lives filled with passion and fulfillment.

A portion of proceeds of this book will help support

To learn more and become involved, visit
www.FrontRowFoundation.org

Proofreading by Tom Skawski II
Foreword by Ben Schemper
Cover sunset image from www.shutterstock.com
Photo in album art on page 62 by Bradley Floden
Photos on pages 124 and 126–128 by SKC Photography

www.CareysPassion.com

ISBN-13 978-0-6925-9938-9

CONTENTS

FOREWORD

Carey Smolensky is a man who truly cares about making a difference in the lives of others. Through his events, collaboration with top thought leaders, and partnerships with impactful businesses and charities, Carey has impacted the lives of tens of thousands of people.

When I first met Carey, I was a young and hungry 18-year-old salesman receiving my first award on stage at a Cutco sales conference. It was one of the most exciting moments of my life thus far, and the experience was one I'll never forget; in part because the event was produced by Carey. Over the next seven years as a Cutco sales leader, I received most of the education, lessons, and leadership that shaped who I am today at conferences, seminars, and events that were put on and produced by the epic and loving man whose book you are reading right now. In my current profession, training top 1% sales leaders, I often share with them that the most powerful element of a learning experience is not the content that you are learning, but the *context* in which you are learning it.

For most of us, the greatest lessons in life were not learned sitting at a desk in a classroom. They were learned through a powerful life experience. I whole-heartedly believe that life experiences are life's greatest teachers, and Carey creates them for a living. Over the years, I have been to hundreds of seminars and conferences, and I've learned that Carey truly is the very best at being the "wizard of Oz" or "the man behind the curtain" that makes it all happen at his events. I've come to love and deeply appreciate just how gifted Carey is at creating powerful contexts for extraordinary learning experiences.

I have been lucky enough to develop a close friendship with Carey beyond our professional relationship. Through our many interactions, I've learned that Carey is a heart-centered, dynamic, passionate man. He lives every day with passion, and positively impacts the lives of anyone who crosses his path. If you've been fortunate enough to cross paths with him, you also know this to be true.

Carey lives congruently in every way. The ideas within this book are not just good advice but instead are "life hacks" being shared from a man who has been intentional in learning from his entire life's journey. The lessons within this book were not learned in a classroom, a seminar, or even in a book. They were downloads Carey received from his many rich relationships, adventures as an entrepreneur, and explorations in passion. I'm excited for you to read the stories and lessons within and receive the gifts of Carey's life experience.

Thank you Carey for being the inspiring and epically impactful man behind this powerful book!

—Ben Schemper

GRATITUDE

I am grateful to my parents for giving me the gifts of life, love, and wisdom. They taught by example and always provided unconditional love. To my father, for serving our country with honor, and, later, demonstrating what dedication and love truly are, by honoring my mother with respect and dignity while caring for her in her final years.

I am grateful to my wife Diane for always supporting me and believing in me. You are the love of my life and I am a better person because of you.

I am grateful to my amazing children, Blake and Rachel. You are each so special in your own ways and I love you both. I am so proud to be your dad and appreciate your support in all that I do. You both give mom and I so much joy.

I am grateful for my Papa for teaching me how to play chess, make the perfect omelet, and to have patience.

I am grateful to Rachel, Trey, Julianna, Todd, Scott, Suzy, Blake, Diane, Teddie, Brendon, Joe, Larry and Jon for sharing your stories with me so that I could use them in my book to inspire the world.

I am grateful to Kosha Dillz, Jay Dillen, L.E. Staiman, PJ, and Brother James who have each collaborated with me to inspire others through our mutual love of creating music to share with the world.

I am grateful to Brent, Shani, John and the rest of our amazing CSP Family: Carey Smolensky Productions, Mobile Music Interactive Entertainment, and STORM Interactive Entertainment. To our producers, entertainers and technical staff, I respect and love you all. Your passion for the work we do allows us to create unforgettable moments and impact the lives of so many.

I am grateful to my friend John Kane, one of the most giving, caring, and selfless people I know. Thank you for who you are, what you stand for, and for impacting the lives of so many. You and the rest of your executive team are second to none.

I am grateful for everyone in my Vector Marketing / Cutco Cutlery extended family all over the world. *It's not about the knives; it's about the lives.* Thank you for being transparent, authentic, and truly some of the most amazing people I am honored to have in my life.

I am grateful to my friends Hal Elrod and Jon Berghoff for providing the clarity at *Best Year Ever BLUEPRINT* to make this book a reality. It is an honor to team with you in impacting lives!

I am grateful to my friend Jon Vroman and all of the selfless, amazing people from Front Row Foundation, who inspire others to live their life in the front row.

I am grateful for my family, friends and clients for your love and support.

I am grateful for all of my raving fans on social media for your likes, follows, and re-tweets on Facebook (Carey's Passion), Instagram (@careyspassion), and Twitter (@careyspassion).

I am grateful to my friend Tom Skawski II, my kindred spirit, for proofing my words like a rockstar. It was a labor of love creating this book and your work will help me to inspire so many.

I am grateful to my friend Ben Schemper for sharing thoughts from his own lens to write the Foreward for my book.

1

EARLY BEGINNINGS / LIFE LESSONS

On December 8, 2014, I was flying back to Chicago after producing a conference for my friends Hal Elrod and Jon Berghoff, called "Best Year Ever BLUEPRINT" in San Diego. It was during this flight that I experienced what I will call a defining moment of clarity.

I was decompressing, and reflecting on my past accomplishments, my recent experiences, and everything that I had recently garnered from the conference. My newly created contacts, combined with the rekindling of past connections gave me a new found energy. This revitalization of my psyche, combined with my new experiences, and conversations with international rap artist, Kosha Dillz, revealed boundless potential, and a multitude of opportunities that I was developing in my mind. As a result, clarity was beginning to emerge. I had always been chasing multiple passions and dreams in different tangents but never focusing on one thing. All of my "wants" came together and suddenly became crystal clear to me. I realized that I would never be truly satisfied with just one thing. I thought, "Were all of my pursuits in vain?" In addition to entertaining and producing, I wanted to pursue my PASSIONS of giving, expressing gratitude, becoming a recording artist, writing my first book, and my desire to pursue professional motivational speaking to inspire others. I have been trying to figure out how to integrate all of my vast experiences and aspirations into one main focus. The focus has always been there, I just had not identified it as a focus; it was PASSION.

According to Albert Einstein, "the definition of insanity is doing the same thing over and over again, but expecting different results." I had been in a rut pursuing my passions without focusing on identifying the bigger picture. Once I gained clarity, I was able to escape from the cycle I had been in. I decided that 2015 was going to be my year of change. Clarity had arrived and I was focused on what I needed to do to create my final transformation. It felt right and I was both excited and anxious to put all of the pieces of this puzzle together.

My friendship with Kosha Dillz began to evolve and we discussed the opportunities of collaborating and performing together in several different performance markets. I realized that I would be able to achieve many of my objectives with one combined effort. The result was my writing and recording a motivational rap song, "With

Your PASSION," featuring Kosha Dillz, which realized one of my dreams of becoming a recording artist early in 2015. The song not only promoted our collaboration, but became another tool in my arsenal for inspiring others. The lyrics call attention to my motivational speaking in that the song represents the way I live my life.

In focusing on what I truly wanted to do with my life, I questioned myself on how I could continue to evolve my family of companies, develop my "passion projects", and expand my gratitude and charitable giving. I took more risks by investing in people to expand my business and when others couldn't step up and do what was needed, I took back the reigns of bringing in business, costing out jobs, and getting back to my old school roots. My Director of Operations, Brent Stringfield, moved to San Diego and we opened our west coast office.

We all know people who are unsatisfied with the work they do. Many do not feel engaged or passionate about what they are doing. Are you one of these people? Are you simply exchanging time for money? Because, if you are, you need to ask yourself, "Is that how I truly want to live my life, when I have a finite amount of time on this earth?"

You must have a goal. If you do not have one, then you are just passing through life as an observer. Goals are usually passion driven, because passion will provide the desire to pursue and achieve the goal. Without passion, the likelihood of falling short, or giving up, is drastically increased. Once you have determined your goal, make sure it is a big one, and then share it with as many people as you can. The action of sharing your goal with others will make you accountable for it. When I decided to write this book, I added the following tag line to my email signature: author of the forthcoming book, "Living Life with PASSION and Helping Others." By doing this, I set in motion the first step in the process of writing, editing, and publishing my first book, even before I had written the very first word. Without a plan, it was only a dream, yet once the plan was announced, I was on my way to making it happen. I had to do it because I said I was going to do it. My word is my bond and my honor. This was my motivation to achieve this goal. It is almost like jumping off a cliff. You can talk about it, but until you take the first leap, you are nowhere closer to doing it.

I think it is only fitting that I am writing this opening portion of my book in a place where I can recall one of my fondest childhood memories. I am poolside at Pheasant Run Resort in St. Charles, IL, one of the many locations that my parents took me on vacation throughout my years growing up. It was here that I remember my father swimming in this very same indoor pool, with me on his back, as I hung onto his shoulders. He turned his head and said to me, "Hang on tight, hold your breath, and keep your head down; we're going under." I didn't have time to think, but I remember taking a deep breath, hanging on, and doing exactly what my father told me to do. When we surfaced, I felt a rush of cold winter air on my head and there was steam rising all around us from the water; we were outside!

I sit here now, over four decades later, gazing at the very same place where my father dove under the separator between the indoor and outdoor pool, with me on his back. It is also the same place that, two decades ago, I shared the same experience with my son, as my father did with me. I am typing these words between the tears that I cannot hold back. The memories of these experiences are so vivid to me, I am able to relive both moments, with fond memories of my dad, my *hero*, who continued to demonstrate his stellar qualities until the day he passed away, as well as remembering these moments with my own son, who is now a grown man, following his dreams and creating a life of his own. The circle of life is real and I am experiencing it in the moment.

I am fortunate to have so many fond memories growing up as an only child. Yes, I'm proud to say it and without any stigma attached. I have never felt as if I was missing out on anything as an only child, and I definitely never had to share my parent's attention with another sibling. Growing up in Wilmette, IL, about 25 miles outside Chicago, my childhood was filled with love, learning by example, hard work, old school ethics, travel and love. Did I mention "love"? Well, it may have been tough love, but I can't stress enough that it was love nonetheless. My parents were amazing people who taught me right from wrong, the benefits of hard work, how to be a mensch (Yiddish for "good person"), to consistently strive for excellence, how to be a gentleman, and to always do the right thing.

I remember, as a young boy, taking a train with my parents to Montreal, Canada to visit my Aunt Jeanne. We were in our hotel room when I screamed, "Mom! Dad! The table's walking into our room!" This was my first experience with room service. I can also remember catching the garter at my cousin Mike Palmer's wedding in California when I was not even 10 years old. I also remember telling my mother, "I wish you had ears so you could hear," while trying to clarify a point I made. Well, my mother thought I said, "I wish you didn't have ears, so you couldn't hear," and what ensued was my mother chasing me around the kitchen table with a wooden spoon. I never talked back to her again, and I never forgot any of these memorable experiences. Memories of our past are imprinted upon our minds forever; some we recall and cherish fondly, while others we may have no recollection of, and are locked away in our subconscious mind.

As I entered high school, a multitude of transformations began to take place in my life. I competed on both the wrestling and swimming teams, became music director of my high school radio station, WNTH-FM, and hosted my own weekly radio show. It was during this time that I developed a passion for music and entertaining, which prompted me to start my own DJ company, Mobile Music Interactive Entertainment. In my senior year, I received the "Golden Mic Award" where I was voted, by my peers, as the high school's favorite DJ.

I was fortunate to have had parents who instilled in me a voracious work ethic. I have always welcomed hard work or any type of challenge, and have never placed limitations on myself based on my perceived physical, mental or emotional abilities. I use the word "perceived" because your state of being is based on your own perception. To this point, I was recently in California with my cousin Mike where he had asked if I wanted to go on a bike ride. He said that we could either do an eighteen mile or a twenty-eight mile ride. I responded by saying, "There is no question, now we must do the twenty-eight mile ride!" I am not one to back down from a challenge, and this was a challenge. It was a beautiful California day, although that may sound redundant, but more importantly, it was an amazing opportunity to spend much sought after time with my cousin. We rode the twenty-eight miles through pristine paths and it is now another one of my memorable life experiences that I have to cherish.

While attending Loyola University of Chicago, I majored in Biology, and lived at home to run my business. I have always worked hard for everything I have ever had in life, and as a result, appreciated it even more. I eventually made enough money from my DJ business to purchase my first car, a 1977 red Trans Am with 6.6 liter engine, hood scoop, and the Firebird emblem on the hood. Of course it was red with a black interior. I was living my dream, a dream that I worked for and never took for granted.

As a freshman, I auditioned at my college radio station, WLUW-FM, for an on-air spot. I soon learned that this was unheard of for a freshman. Students would "normally" intern at the station for years before even thinking about getting their own show and, if they were lucky, they might be fortunate enough to have a show by their senior year.

I was awarded my own prime time slot! Countless students were studying to go into broadcasting, and here I was doing it as a hobby, a passion, that I enjoyed. Several months later, the radio station's format changed from Top 40 to News Talk, so I reinvented myself. In addition to anchoring the news and recording PSAs (Public Service Announcements), I created a talk show called "Comedy Showcase" where, along with my very own sidekick, we ROCKED the airwaves with a hilarious, old school comedy show and even had a "joke hotline"!

Throughout my college career, I took advantage of everything my school, and life, had to offer. I went for it all! I was voted Class President each year, DJ-ed my weekly radio show, became a P.A.D.I. certified Scuba Diver through the R.O.T.C., represented my college in Israel for the JUF/UJA Annual Campaign, and in 1984 competed in and became the first Mr. United States (male version of the Miss America Pageant) in Long Beach, CA, where I traveled across the country making television appearances on shows like The Phil Donahue Show and escorting celebrities like Heather Locklear. Decades after catching the garter at his wedding, my cousin Mike was in the audience watching me win my title. To top it off, I met the love of my life while DJ-ing her father's 50th surprise birthday party. Not bad for a college experience. Did I mention I was majoring in biology?

Had I truly followed my passion earlier in life, I might have taken a different academic path. I truly believe that who we are is a result of the culmination of our life's experiences. If I had to do it all over again, I would not want to make my journey easier; however I would have followed my heart instead of my brain. I have since learned to live with passion and follow my heart. I love what I do and wake up each day inspired to make a difference in not only my business, and in people's lives, but in the world as well. Intellectually, I do not regret any of my decisions in life as they have all contributed to building my character to make me the man I am today.

I graduated as a Bachelor of Science in biology and although I have never used my degree, college afforded me opportunities to constantly challenge myself to make the most out of every waking minute I had. I learned to adapt to change rather than resist it, and to go after anything I wanted. If you don't try, you won't succeed, so you might as well try and give it your all. You will never regret having tried, but you will forever regret not trying. Whenever I was not studying or working, I was constantly pursuing and exploring new passions and opportunities.

My parents provided me with so many character building lessons that helped shape me into the man that eventually married my amazing wife, Diane. From that point on, I have grown, together with my wife, to constantly become a better person, a better husband, and a better father. I have learned from my children as well, and the process continues to evolve.

It is said that the best way to teach is by example. As a parent, I am proud that both of my children have learned to not only identify their passions, but to truly follow and live them. My daughter, Rachel, has summed this up in the following way, "How many people have the ability to wear the hat of an entrepreneur, an entertainer, a producer, an actor, an author, a recording artist, and a motivational speaker? This incredibly diversified person is my exceptional father, Carey Smolensky. When I was a little girl my father and I coined the phrase, 'same face, same taste.' Not only does my appearance resemble his, but so does my drive in life to live each day to its fullest. Climbing up a waterfall, rock climbing, zip lining, scuba diving, and rappelling down a 27-story building are each examples of how my dad has taught me to adventurously live my life with passion."

Rachel reflected on her process, "Growing up, I continuously pondered what I would be when I grew up. After many short-lived ideas, I embraced my lifelong passion of teaching children. As an elementary school teacher, my journey as an educator is constantly evolving, one child at a time. One of my favorite quotes is, *'Teachers who love teaching, teach children to love learning.'* If I was not passionate about the content I taught, then I could not expect my students to enjoy learning. That being said, it is essential for me to enthusiastically empower our youth to learn each and every day."

I share these stories with you because these are the experiences that continue to shape my passions today, as well as who I am and what I stand for. How many times have you smelled an apple pie and immediately thought of your grandmother's house, or tasted old-fashioned lemonade that triggered a memory of a particular hot summer day? We have been imprinted with experiences throughout our life, some good and some bad. Regardless, they are all experiences that have had a significant impact on the person we are today.

One of the very first lessons I learned from my parents was to always tell the truth and to always be accountable for my actions. I remember coming home from high school one day, and my parents were sitting at the kitchen table waiting for me. By the look on their faces, I knew something was up. My father started telling me how concerned they were about me and he showed me a syringe that he had found in our house. He had taken it to a pharmacist who verified that it was indeed a real one, and when a hypodermic needle was attached, it is used for injecting drugs.

As soon as I saw the packaged needle in my father's hand, I felt a pit in my stomach and had flashbacks from years ago as a little boy. I remembered seeing a drawer full of these syringes when I was at my pediatrician's office and innocently took one, thinking how cool it would have been to use as a squirt gun. There was no needle attached, it was just the plastic part still sealed in its sterile wrapper. I remembered coming home from the doctor's office that day and hiding it in our downstairs bathroom behind the toilet paper and tissues. I had forgotten about the syringe until that very moment years later, when I saw it in my dad's hands. When I realized what my father was holding, the entire scenario came back to me so vividly, and I was impacted by the realization of what my parent's perception was of that situation. I felt terrible that they had to go through the mental anguish earlier that day, facing the possibility that their son could have been using drugs. After explaining the whole story to my parents, and apologizing for what my actions had put them through, we hugged, cried and event laughed, and then chalked it up to me being a kid.

The lessons I have learned throughout life have evolved into what

I call a "no-excuses mindset." Each of us has all of the tools that are needed to become the best version of ourselves at any point in time, regardless of age or circumstance. Most people spend the first half of their lives thinking they are too young to do things, and the second half of their lives thinking they are too old to do them. Young people will rationalize about not having enough experience, while the older generation reflects on running out of time. Stay away from limiting excuses like, "you can't teach an old dog new tricks." I believe you can, it just depends on the dog's passion. Have an open mind, be willing to learn, and throw away your excuses. Excuses like an actor thinking, "I'm not as talented," or a sales person believing, "I don't have the right territory." Don't spend your life dealing with excuses. Believe in yourself and know that you have what it takes.

You need to persevere and find the right opportunities in life, because if you don't, chances are that they will not find you. If you really don't have what it takes at a particular moment in time, then "fake it till you make it." Keep moving towards your goals and never look back. I remember when I started my DJ business and, as a young teenager, I was looked down upon by adults as 'just a kid.' Some people thought, "how could this punk know anything about entertaining adults?" I never let this perceived obstacle stand in my way because, once people saw my talents in reading a crowd, my vocal skills on the mic, combined with my vast knowledge of every genre of music, my age no longer mattered. Do things for yourself, follow your passion, don't wait for handouts, and never wait for others to make things happen for you. If you wait, you will never realize your dreams. What people say to you, or what others do to you, does not have the power to affect you unless you give it the power to allow it to affect you. Similarly, fast-forward almost four decades to the present when a 12-year-old finds out that the DJ for their Bar Mitzvah is the same DJ that did their dad's Bar Mitzvah or even their parents' wedding. Imagine the horror that that child is anticipating, only to find that I completely rock their celebration along with my amazing dancers, beatboxers, percussionists and world-class entertainers. Fortunately, we have videos to show how awesome we are, and no child ever has to imagine that horror. But I digress...

Age is something that, if you let it, can be limiting and will set boundaries for you. I believe that age is irrelevant in work as long as you have the passion for your craft and you can deliver above people's expectations. In life, I believe that, as with age, your appreciation of experiences is heightened because you have experienced so much and therefore have a broader frame of reference. The timeless adage, "act your age," is actually offensive to me. Who reserves the right to actually determine how anyone should act at any age? I feel like I am still in my 20s, so why should I act like someone who may be in their 50s and feel like they are in their 70s? It makes no sense to me because most of my friends and business associates are twenty years my junior and, oftentimes, I sleep less, work harder and have more energy than they do. I recently spent three hours on an intensive zip line and ropes course in upstate New York. My 28-year-old buddy only lasted through one of the beginning levels and was done. I don't mean done as in finished; I mean he was DONE. I'm not going to tell you who he is, because I don't want to call him out. But when Jordan (oops) left to go back to the lodge, I continued on for over two more hours, challenging myself on different courses ending with the Black Widow Diamond course. This is how I choose to live my life. Anything I do, I push myself as hard as I can and the rewards are immeasurable.

It is important to point out that intergenerational relationships are mutually beneficial. One can argue the point that any relationship can be mutually beneficial, and I agree. However, most young people don't always realize this until they are older, and older people usually are not interested in developing relationships with younger generations because they are either set in their ways, may feel threatened, or just cannot fathom what they would have in common. I believe if people were more open-minded, everyone would benefit and each of us has something valuable to contribute to help others.

I have found, from having entertained over a million people, that the majority of people over 40 tend to be stuck in a musical time warp from when they last danced in college. This is not a bad thing and of course there are exceptions to the rule. The exceptions are usually the Type-A personalities, like me, who are constantly expanding their musical knowledge and tend to get bored with listening to the same thing all the time. Most people like what they like and are comfortable with their preferences in music. Only when they have children do they listen to current music, and not by choice. One of my close friends, Gary Gillis, is a huge YES fan, and although I have gone with Gary to a few YES concerts and can appreciate their music, it never ceases to amaze me that if Gary had his choice, YES would be all that he would listen to. I respect the fact that this is his passion, because, "who am I to question or judge anyone else's passion?" Each of us should find their own passion regardless of what other people think of it.

You need to share your passions in order to make them real, and if you want something bad enough, then go for it and don't let anything or anyone stand in your way. With passion and perseverance, you can become unstoppable. Learn from your setbacks, and when you fall, which you inevitably will, get back up and keep going. Most of us have had bad things happen to us, but these things do not define us. Rather, we must learn from these experiences and, as a result, become stronger. Furthermore, if you dwell on these negative experiences, they will distance you from your ultimate purpose and goal. Use the amazing abilities and power that you have within you to overcome obstacles and to follow your passions. We have all had setbacks, been hurt by others, and encountered roadblocks that have tried to derail us from our ultimate path. We need to get past the roadblocks and not allow them to control our future. Decide to live your life with passion right now, regardless of your current situation because life is too short to settle for anything less than you deserve. Each day is a new beginning, filled with new opportunities and new perspectives. We will always encounter people who are negative about our goals, or who dismiss what we choose to do, so do it anyway! A positive mindset is the first step towards achieving and fulfilling your passions. A positive attitude will define your destiny.

With the practice of positive thinking, your subconscious will eventually believe this as true.

Decide now to have a "no excuses" mindset. Don't think about excuses and don't speak to others about your excuses. More importantly, you need to change your mindset and know that you can do it. Believe in yourself, and in your own unique abilities, fully believing that you are enough. You are capable of accomplishing whatever you set out to do. It is never too late to live a life filled with passion, whatever your age, as long as you have a positive mindset and are determined to pursue your passion without giving up.

Be accountable for the situation you are presently in, and if you are not living the life of your dreams, or one that you are passionate about, then do something to change your situation. Resist the urge to make excuses or to blame others for your current situation. Make this your number one task and do something each day to facilitate that change. Each of us can control, to some extent, the influences that surround us. We choose our circle of friends, who we interact with in and of our work, what we spend money on, and most importantly, our own perception of the life we live.

2

OLD SCHOOL RULES

I believe that people in every generation affectionately reflect upon their younger years as "the good ol' days". For me, these were the days when we had rotary dial phones, were taught cursive writing, and had recess breaks in school. It was a time before we had microwaves, fax machines, and even the internet. It was also a time when schools, malls, and movie theatres were safe. I believe in "the good ol' days," it was easier for people to live a life of passion simply because we had fewer distractions.

People used to interact with each other with "real" face time! Yes, actually conversing face-to-face, with pure, uninterrupted, high-quality one-on-one time. With technology advancing faster with every passing minute, and apps that can do more and more,

I often find solace in reminiscing upon a simpler time when we seemed to experience real life as opposed to a virtual one. If we are not careful, these "old school" skills may soon be gone forever: letter writing, cooking from scratch, sewing, proper spelling and grammar, map reading, remembering phone numbers, and even meeting people without the aid of the internet.

THE TRIVIALIZATION OF THE ENGLISH LANGUAGE

My mother spoke six languages (English, German, Yiddish, Spanish, Polish and Russian) and I pride myself in my own command of the English language, while in the constant pursuit of achieving excellence in communicating. It is truly a shame that in our great country, there is a staggering amount of people who, even after going through our educational systems, still have not mastered the English language. Then there are some people who *do* have a mastery of the language, but have a blatant disregard for its proper usage. Imagine a driver swerving from one lane to another, then making a U-turn across yellow lines, and then start traveling in the opposite direction and then turn around against oncoming traffic that would be a similar scenario to the conversations that I have had with people who begin their sentence or reply with, "I mean", or "you know" or "it's like" or "ya know I mean". No, I have no clue as to what you mean!

Now, as a DJ, recording artist, and member of the entertainment community, I pride myself in appreciating all styles of music. I also understand the use of rap slang and other colloquialisms in music writing and song. In 2015, I released my first rap song, "With Your PASSION", featuring Kosha Dillz: I too used slang, but in the context of the artistry of the song (shameless plug: available in all digital stores worldwide). What becomes frustrating, and oftentimes infuriating, is when people, because of their ignorance (not necessarily their lack of knowledge) intentionally misuse grammar thinking it's "cool". They use language in a manner that disrespects themselves without their even knowing it. To be successful, respected, and to be taken seriously in the business community, one cannot use phrases such as, "like", "I mean", or "ya know", when starting a sentence. It is a ridiculous colloquialism, and one that has somehow gained acceptance in younger generations. There are people I know as friends or family that intentionally choose to exhibit this behavior and I have come to realize that it's really not my business to give them my opinion, unless they ask for it. Even when asked, people don't always want to hear the truth. They want to hear whatever reinforces their own beliefs, and if the requested assessment is not in direct alignment with their own perspective, then the conversation will not go well. Some people will get highly offended, shut down, and even stop listening, thinking you are out of touch when you try to make them aware of their own actions. The reality is that it grates at my inner core to listen to that nonsense. I subscribe to an app that emails me a different word, with definition, and pronunciation, every day. Learning should be a lifetime process and I believe it is the laziness of some people, despite their generation, that allows this trivialization to continually occur.

Andrew Aitken "Andy" Rooney was an American radio and television writer, best known for his weekly broadcast "A Few Minutes with Andy Rooney," a part of the CBS News program *60 Minutes* from 1978 to 2011. When I was growing up, I remember watching this program with my parents and listening to Andy Rooney's weekly rant and thought it was not only interesting, sarcastic, and entertaining, but had an underlining seriousness to it. Use of the English language has only gotten worse over the years and I think, were Andy Rooney still alive, that he would have been proud of my assessment.

CHIVALRY

In today's relaxed culture, where people text each other to hook up, it seems that chivalry is rare indeed. Have people lost their ability to communicate? People don't take the time to develop a relationship and get to know each other anymore. Chivalry emerged as the natural progression of treating women with respect. Some say that chivalry is dead. I almost succumbed to that notion while my daughter was dating, until she finally met her husband. Holding open a door, pulling out a chair, offering your jacket, walking on the outside (closest to the street), and paying for dinner are all gestures, I believe, that show respect to women, and in no way are meant to offend women. Unfortunately, the more I look around, the less I see men treating women the way I believe women should be treated. I remember my father always bringing home gladiolas, roses, mums, and birds of paradise (his favorite) for my mother during all of the holidays and at any celebration. As a result, I have carried on the same tradition in our own home. Are flowers and chocolates a thing of the past? I say no, not if you live your life with passion.

Growing up, I never knew anyone who was divorced. Now, one out of every two marriages ends in divorce. Marital problems like infidelity, financial stress, abuse, and even differences of opinion in how to raise children can remove the spark of romance and increase a couple's overall stress level. Too many people give up when the going gets tough. Old school rules dictate fixing something that is broken, rather than throwing it away. I believe this applies to marriage as well as anything in life of value. I am proud to be married to my bride, the love of my life, for almost 28 years.

ETIQUETTE

The original etiquette manuals of Western civilization were actually success manuals. As author Steven Pinker notes, they taught knights and nobles how to conduct themselves in the court of the king; which is where we get the concepts of "courtly" and "courtesy." My parents taught me the value of proper etiquette at a young age and raised me to be a gentleman. I remember my parents taking me on trips when I was a child, and we would get dressed up just to go on an airplane. It was a simpler time back then, a more respectful, proper, and more formal era. It was a time when people respected themselves as well as each other. A man wanted to impress his lady, and cared about his own looks, clothing, and style. Ladies acted like ladies, at least in public, and one's own reputation was something to be valued. Some people may interpret these standards as being chauvinistic. Let me assure you that they are not. On the contrary, they are what I would term as being classy and respectful. The resurgence of old school attire, made mainstream in pop culture by the artist

Macklemore in the song, "Thrift Shop" includes these lyrics:

> I'm a take your grandpa's style, I'm a take your grandpa's style,
> No for real – ask your grandpa – can I have his hand-me-downs?
> (Thank you)

HONOR & RESPECT

In any generation, ethics, honesty, and honor matter! They are reflections of who we are, and represent what each of us stands for. It is what truly matters in our lives. Once there is honor, there is righteousness and integrity. By having honor, moral values are achieved, truth will prevail, and virtue is realized.

Children should be taught to respect their elders. Respect focuses on manners as well as proper behavior in the presence of others. While I believe we should respect our elders, we should also respect each other, regardless of age. Showing respect to others honors the other person. There is also great value in being a person of honor, and to inherently know the difference between right and wrong. These are absolutes and are not open to interpretation. A good rule to practice is to always do the right thing even when no one is watching. It is crucial to understand:

> *Right is right even if nobody is doing it.*
> *Wrong is wrong even if everyone is doing it.*

Old school values and teachings are needed now more than ever.

With the continual acts of violence within our society, people are becoming increasingly desensitized to the daily images and stories that we see and hear about murder, terrorism, war, and destruction. Random acts of violence are on the rise and the lack of respect for human life threatens the moral fabric of our society as a whole.

COMMITMENT

Abraham Lincoln said, "Commitment is what transforms a promise into reality." While I agree with this statement describing the *process* of commitment, it does not address the *emotion* of it. For example, when we commit to something, we are in a particular mood, or state of emotion, based on the circumstances of that very moment. The act of keeping one's word and remaining loyal to what you have pledged beyond that point is where commitment comes in. Whenever I commit to do anything, I am all in. As I mentioned earlier, my word is my bond and my honor.

On a seemingly normal day, I went to Chicago's O'Hare International airport to fly to Atlanta, Georgia for my friend Trey's wedding. He wanted me to personally DJ his wedding and I was honored to do so. I arrived at the airport early Friday morning for my 7:30 am flight when I soon learned that my flight had been cancelled. I travel quite a bit and am used to changes, so I worked on getting on to the next flight and was confirmed. The wedding was not until Saturday night, so I still had plenty of time.

Then I received notification that my new flight was canceled. Not knowing why, I scrambled to get on the next flight out, and it was cancelled while I was speaking with the agent. There were only two more flights scheduled, but by now ALL scheduled flights on the departure board had been cancelled.

Not only did Trey want me to perform at his wedding, but I had given him my word that I would be there. After evaluating all of my options such as other airports, trains, and even a bus, I realized that, although I was able to get booked on a 9:30 pm flight, scheduled to arrive in Atlanta before midnight, there was still no guarantee that flights would resume by then. My only option was to drive there.

After seeing all of the other passengers waiting for their luggage, some for up to 4 hours...I quickly changed my course of action. I found a supervisor, expressed the urgency of my predicament and asked for his help. Tommy Gushes, Duty Manager of American Airlines was amazing. Around 1 pm I received a call from Tommy that my bags would be on the luggage turnstile in about 5 minutes.

The point I have yet to mention is the reason for all of the cancellations. This was the day that someone set fire to the FAA radar center, grounding more than 2,000 flights in Chicago. Everyone was frantically trying to get their luggage, rent vehicles and get out any way they could. My son-in-law happens to be a manager at Enterprise Rent-A-Car and he was able to book me a one-way full size car, so with luggage in tow, I was on the road to Atlanta by 1:20 pm.

After a 13-hour drive, and the loss of an hour due to the time change, I arrived at my hotel at 3:30 am, unpacked, set several alarms and wake up calls and slept for six hours (4–10 am). I attended the pre-wedding brunch and DJ-ed the wedding.

There were many points throughout this journey that I could

have given up, or resorted to an easier way out. After all, I did have a valid excuse. These choices were not an option for me, as I never look for the easy way out and I despise excuses. It is by this code of honor that I live my life. Trey honored me with a testimonial, "Carey Smolensky is a very rare breed: an amazing artist, compassionate husband, benevolent father, and dear friend. Whether it is a corporate retreat in the largest stadium, a wedding for friends, or any gathering, Carey delivers by leading with his heart and always asking what he can do to make the world a better place. He is proof that something greater is out there calling us all to action."

FORGIVENESS

Most of us can remember having been hurt by someone in our past. We may have been hurt emotionally, or physically, but either way, it was, and still is, painful. Maybe it happened to us on the bus, in school, at a dance, or even at the playground. Whatever the scenario, we often recall the situation with impeccable detail. When we think of the person who caused the hurt, we remember them from the way we felt about them at that very moment. The situation may have occurred decades ago, but the pain has not gone away if we have yet to forgive the person. While pain is normal, if we allow the pain to linger for too long, we will keep reliving the pain over and over. We get trapped in a cycle of anger and hurt, and miss out on being present in life.

I believe that forgiveness is truly a noble act. By definition, forgiveness is the intentional and voluntary process by which a victim undergoes a change in feelings and attitude regarding an offense, while letting go of negative emotions such as vengefulness, with an increased ability to wish the offender well.

At its core, forgiveness is an acknowledgment that a person who has harmed us still has the capacity for good. You don't have to wait to get an apology from someone in order to grant that person forgiveness. When you forgive someone, it doesn't condone their actions, or erase the past; it simply frees you from being their eternal victim and allows you to move on with your life and be happy. Forgiveness can truly change your life.

The process of forgiving another person takes time. You must first commit to making the change and to let go of grudges. Grudges not only create stress, but serve to allow negative events from your past undermine your happiness of today and, in turn, your future. You need to realize that the pain is hurtful to you, and can even be stopping you from pursuing your own passions. Your happiness is far more important than harboring anger. Although you cannot control the actions of other people, you have the power of choice and can decide to move on.

After forgiving someone, feel empathy for the person and only wish peace and love for them. Do not revisit the past, just focus on the present, and go forward in happiness. Remember to *love* not *hate*.

BE MEMORABLE

Phineas Taylor "P. T." Barnum, founder of the Barnum & Bailey Circus, said, "Without promotion, something terrible happens... Nothing!" I believe that if you are passionate about what you do in life, others will take notice. At a recent event I was producing, an attendee came up to me and said, "sorry for being awkward but, you always look good when you come to conferences – you look like a rock star!" I thanked him for the compliment and walked off like a rock star. Another person told a new Facebook friend from our group, "Wait until it's your birthday, Carey does something very cool with your picture!" This comment refers to me posting digitally enhanced themed images for my friends on their birthdays. I want people to know that I care about them and I try to do more than just text them on their special day. I try to not treat people like I want to be treated, but rather how *they* want to be treated. No matter what, make a positive impact on others. As Maya Angelou said, "I've learned that people will forget what you said, people will forget what you did, but people will never forget how you made them feel."

Making someone else feel good is naturally one of the easiest things you can do. A smile does not cost anything, and a compliment goes a long way. Sometimes we get so caught up in ourselves that we forget to acknowledge others. Remember to be present and in the moment whenever you are in the presence of someone else.

Here are a few "old school rules" that I believe to be timeless:

- Respect your elders (and everyone else).

- No means no!

- Never order a more expensive meal than the person paying for the meal.

- Always say "please" and "thank you".

- Always keep your word.

- Always give a strong handshake and look the other person in the eye.

- Remove your hat when appropriate.

- Learn how to eat with chopsticks.

- Learn how to tie a real bow tie.

- Know how to cook one dish perfectly.

- Always wear polished shoes and a classy wristwatch.

- Arrive 15 minutes early; on time is late.

- Be confident; it's sexy.

- Know how to set a proper table.

- Always do the right thing, even when no one is watching.

- Always have a nice pen.

- Hold the door open for the person behind you.

Living a life of passion, to me, is an overall state of being. It is an appreciation of life; to enjoy each moment, appreciate what we have, and follow our dreams. This state of being is timeless and is not exclusive to any generation or era.

3

FINDING YOUR PASSION

Do you ever feel like there is something is missing in your life? Maybe you want to make a difference in the world in which you live, but you believe it is impossible. You are not alone, because so many of us walk through life, feeling lost and desperate in search of a deeper purpose, and not knowing how to find it. As we travel through this journey called life, we are faced with a variety of stages of personal growth and development. Throughout our life our true passions inevitably define who we are destined to become. Sometimes things are revealed to us throughout our life that allows us to understand and realize what we truly desire, or how to get to the next level of fulfillment. I will refer to these levels, or stages, as job, career, and calling.

As most of us begin our adult life, we focus on getting a job that allows us to make money in order to support ourselves, and eventually our family. This, in turn, leads to a career that we, ideally, either have a passion to pursue and devote a large amount of our life to, or leads us to another career that better fits our needs and lifestyle. Finally, there is the realization of our true calling, which provides purpose and self-fulfillment in our lives.

It is easy to be so focused on whatever stage we are currently in, such that we never look beyond, to explore the possibilities of something greater. This is necessary in order to achieve a higher level of personal purpose and fulfillment. Two of the most impactful days of your life are the day you were born, and the day you determine what your passion is. The day you were born was not only your introduction into this amazing world, but the start of your life journey. If you go through life without ever determining what your passion is, then you will continue to feel unfulfilled, and will never determine your true calling. Many people, who are solely driven by money throughout their lives in order to leave a legacy for their family, in their elder years, often regret their decisions, as they still feel unfulfilled. The dictionary defines legacy as an amount of money or property left to someone in a will. I believe that legacy is more about sharing what you have *learned*, not what you have *earned*. It is also about bequeathing values over valuables.

It was not until I removed myself from my daily routine and immersed myself in a truly motivational and inspirational experience that I was able to focus on and determine my true calling. This experience gave me time to reflect and realize that all of the passions I had could all be directed into a common focus, and that focus was indeed passion itself.

In that life defining flight back home from San Diego, finding my true calling became crystal clear. I had been passionate about so many things, and even to be as bold as to say, proficient at just about all of them. I found that my vast experiences had led me to be overqualified for so many of the things that I was doing that I was no longer finding them challenging. I have, for as long as I can remember, wanted to continually evolve and to challenge myself, pushing myself to my limits in everything I do.

While pursuing the numerous passions in my life, I have identified my own stages of personal growth and development in the following ways. My *job* can be identified in three ways. I work as an event producer, DJ / emcee, and interactive entertainer.

My *career* can be summed up in several ways. I am the founder and president of my family of companies: Carey Smolensky Productions, CSP Worldwide, Mobile Music Interactive Entertainment, STORM Interactive Entertainment, and CSP Video. I am also Executive Vice President of my wife's company, Custom Specialty Promotions.

While on my flight from San Diego I discovered my true *calling*: to inspire, to help, and to motivate others in order to change lives. Writing this book, along with motivational speaking, and creating social media communities on Facebook (Carey's Passion), Instagram (careyspassion), and Twitter (careyspassion) are the first steps, of many, in pursuing my calling to inspire others.

START NOW

In the words of Henry David Thoreau, "Most men lead lives of quiet desperation and go to the grave with the song still in them." Most people spend the first half of their lives thinking they are too young to do something, and the second half of their lives thinking they are too old to do it. Rather than deliberating on all the ways to get started, and what process you should follow, just start now. To quote Nike's famous slogan, "Just do it." It is very easy to succumb to the process of planning in your mind and visualizing what will happen while making excuses as to why it is not the right time to do it now.

Change is not easy; if it were easy, everyone would do it. Too many people pass on opportunities such as having a child, moving to a new home, changing jobs or even writing a book because they are either afraid of change or may not feel it is the right time. Rationalization is nothing more than a self-defeating stalling technique. It is easier to believe that we will pursue our objectives when we have more money, more time, or even more experience. If we wait for the right time, it will never come. There is no guarantee of what tomorrow will bring, so if we want to make something happen, we need to take action today.

If you find yourself questioning the process, you are overthinking it. Children can find great happiness in pretending to be whoever or whatever they want to be. Whether a firemen, an astronaut, a racecar driver, a Super Bowl quarterback, brain surgeon, millionaire or even the President of the United States. Why is it that as adults we have often lost this ability and have placed limitations on our imagination? This is a process that did not happen overnight, but rather is the result of a lack of encouragement from parents, teachers and even people who have not found their own passions, and secretly live a life of quiet desperation. Learn from the innocence of children and do not be afraid to expand your vision; explore new experiences and find out what really excites you. It is amazing to see the results that start to emerge after simply choosing to get started.

IDENTIFY THE THINGS YOU LIKE AND DISLIKE

The first thing to do is to surround yourself with things in life that you enjoy and give you happiness while removing negative influences that hold you back from achieving your true greatness. Ask yourself, "What truly gives me happiness?" Start exploring these passions and be aware of where these inspirations are coming from. At the same time, identify the things in your life that give you anxiety, frustration and seem to drain your energy. There is much more to life than just living it, and life can be an amazing journey filled with inspiration, beauty and contentment if we follow our passions. Embrace this process, and after reviewing the list you have created, work on integrating the positive items into your life on a daily basis and slowly remove and avoid the negatives that do not allow you to be the best version of yourself.

> "Do what you need to do until you can choose to do what you want to do."
> —Carey Smolensky

BE NEG ON NEGATIVITY

Just as positive people are attracted to positive energy, negative people are attracted to negative energy. Your unconscious beliefs can make you into a negative person without you even being aware of it. In the words of the Dalai Lama, "When you think everything is someone else's fault, you will suffer a lot. When you realize that everything springs only from yourself, you will learn both peace and joy." Negativity will only breed weakness while a positive mental attitude is unstoppable. Be mentally tough and don't allow negative things or negative people to distract your focus. Creating a positive mental attitude allows for positive thoughts and an optimistic perspective that dramatically increases the desired outcome of the task at hand.

Have confidence in yourself and abandon any negative and self-limiting attitudes you have. Examples of these attitudes are, "I'm not good enough," "I can't do it," or even "I don't deserve to be happy." Regardless of the misfortunes I have had in my life, I try to maintain the perspective of always looking at the glass as half full, rather than half empty. This has allowed me to be objective and not only learn from my past challenges, but also understand that a negative perspective is always self-defeating.

By developing a positive mental attitude, and emphasizing strong and confident attitudes and beliefs, you become mentally prepared to handle any challenge. In the words of Henry Ford, "Whether you believe you can or cannot do something, either way you are correct." Understand and believe that each of us is here for a specific purpose.

Each of us is truly unique in this world, with a unique fingerprint, heartbeat, and thought process unlike anyone else that has ever lived or that has yet to be born. Know and believe that you have something amazing to offer this world and there are other people that can benefit by you sharing your gifts with humanity.

If you are complaining about your current situation or about things that have happened in your life, then you are sending out negative energy, and therefore attracting negativity. Positive people will avoid you, as they naturally try to avoid bringing negativity into their own lives. A positive mental attitude gives you the courage to believe in yourself and, although you may fail time and time again, it will also give you the courage to keep getting up until you succeed. There are many techniques to enhance positive mental attitude such as daily affirmations, surrounding yourself with positive and inspirational people, motivational podcasts, recorded books, and even journaling. There is no right or wrong, do whatever works best for you. Once you have made positive changes in your life, while simultaneously removing the negativity, your perspective will begin to change and you will start attracting other positive people.

BREAK UP WITH THE "ONE"

Many of us struggle because we try to find that ONE thing that we are destined for. We go to college to find the one major that will define us, or the profession that will bring us happiness for the rest of our lives. I believe that our perception of what we are destined for is constantly evolving and, for that reason, trying to find the one thing keeps us in a cycle similar to a dog trying to chase its tail. Life has so many opportunities that pursuing the one thing can only limit us from finding our true potential and eventually our true calling. Take me for example: I have multiple family roles, job titles and hobbies. I'm a husband, father, event producer, DJ, emcee, entertainer, author, speaker, recording artist, actor, rescue diver and lover of extreme sports. I enjoy everything that I do. Although they all bring me fulfillment, none of these solely define me or my purpose, as some are jobs, while others are family roles. However each role is also a passion of mine. I have found by living a life with passion, that is when you truly feel alive.

Conventional education and institutions prepare us for the one thing we think we want to do in life. The widely touted theory, highlighted in a 1993 psychology paper and popularized by Malcolm Gladwell's book *Outliers*, says that anyone can master a skill with 10,000 hours of practice, give or take. I believe that innate talent, along with age, life experience and the level of deliberate practice are also considerations in one's ability to master a skill. Regardless of your level of ability or proficiency, what if there were more things you were called to do in life, other than the one you are currently doing or pursuing? You will never know unless you expand your horizons and constantly challenge yourself to experience new things. We stop resisting the unknown because of fear and we fully engage in experiencing every moment of the amazing life that we have been blessed with. Living a passion filled life, *daily,* leaves no room for questioning your purpose because your purpose starts to become self-evident, as you begin to live a fulfilling life.

LIVE IN THE PRESENT

"Yesterday's the past, tomorrow's the future, but today is a gift. That's why it's called the present." – Bil Keane

I believe that anything you do in life should be done with laser focus. The human brain is not wired for multitasking. We have all heard the time-honored expression of not being able to walk and chew gum at the same time. In today's fast-paced society, with continual technological advances, multitasking seems to have become the norm. Lord Chesterfield, in one of the many letters he wrote to his son in the 1740s, gave the following advice: "There is enough for everything, in the course of the day, if you do but one thing at once; but there is not time enough in the year, if you will do two things at a time." Chesterfield went on to explain, "This steady and undissipated attention to one object is a sure mark of a superior genius; as hurry, bustle, and agitation are the never-failing symptoms of a weak and frivolous mind." He believed that singular focus was not merely a practical way to structure one's time, but a mark of intelligence.

Multitasking may give the appearance of allowing us to be more efficient in completing tasks, however, we lose the fulfillment of being fully engaged with the primary task at hand. Whether it is a conversation with another person, driving a vehicle, or operating heavy machinery, if you are not fully engaged, you are not executing these tasks to your full potential or to the potential needed to complete the job well. While in a conversation, if you are texting, looking around the room, or thinking about what's going to be happening later that day, you are not only disrespecting the person you are speaking to, but you are also not engaging with that person to your utmost potential. We have all spoken to someone on the phone and realized, by the tone of the conversation, that the other person is reading emails, texting, or multitasking in other ways. If you are driving a vehicle and are not completely focused because you are texting, eating, or programming your GPS, it only takes a fraction of a second for a pedestrian to run in front of your car or for you not to see another vehicle turning into your lane. In that fraction of a second, your life, along with the lives of others, can be altered forever. As a result, laws have been changed making usage of cell phones and other electronic devices while driving, illegal. Focus 100% on the task at hand because focus is powerful. Laser focus is unstoppable!

In the blog of the business section of the Huffington Post (10/23/15), Alison A. Quirk wrote about the *Myth of Multitasking*: "As if the fear of missing out isn't reason enough to explain our device addiction, it has a corollary, too: the idea that we can focus our attention on several things at once. In a world of countless screens and news feeds vying for our attention, we've convinced ourselves that multitasking isn't just something that's possible, it's a virtue. However, research shows that multitasking is a myth. It is performance-destroying, not performance-enhancing. It divides our attention, splits our focus and spreads us too thinly."

I'd like to point out that these are, in fact, predominantly first world problems. I can remember traveling with my wife and children for many years to Jamaica and each time being envious of the people living on the beach, in a hut, in paradise with not a care in the world. I used to comment on the irony of working hard all year to be able to afford a 10-day trip, just to experience what the locals experience all year round. The more complex our lives have become, the more challenging it is to live each day with passion unless we make it a priority. It is easy to be focused on the next big thing while we are neglecting the present. To truly experience anything in full, you must be 100% engaged. The past cannot be changed, the future has yet to unfold, and the present is all we truly have to experience. When you are fully engaged in the present, and experiencing the moment completely, without expectations, whatever you are doing is that much more fulfilling.

Expectations, or rather unrealistic expectations, detract from truly experiencing life in the moment. According to Miranda Morris, Ph.D., a clinical psychologist in Bethesda, MD, "It's part of the human experience." Unrealistic expectations can tarnish relationships, undermine our goals, and can even set us up for failure. Always keep an open mind, as you never know what opportunities will unfold, whom you will meet, or where life will take you.

SPEND TIME WITH YOURSELF

It is said that patience is a virtue, and if that is true, then one of society's biggest vices has to be impatience. How often have you been upset that your laptop is taking too long to start, a traffic light is taking too long to change, or how furious you become when a person is driving too slowly in front of you?

Growing up, we often think that our parents are disconnected, out of touch, and don't really understand what we are going through.

The older we get, the more we tend to realize, and contrary to our earlier beliefs, that our parents were much wiser than we first anticipated. They did the very best they could with the tools they were given. It is also important to understand that everyone was young once and we all experienced growing pains in one form or another. Although times and technology may be different, we all have experienced very similar emotions and feelings throughout our lives.

For as much as I love technology and can't wait for the next new concept to be released, I truly enjoy being unplugged. I have found solace in the times when I am on a plane, where I can be, or choose to be, disconnected from the rest of the world, even if just for a few hours. It is here that I can focus, without interruption. A testament to this is that I have written a good portion of this book while traveling or being unplugged from communicative technology. I have found that this solace can also be achieved by the following call to action.

Every day, spend time alone with yourself, slowing down, tuning off the outside world, listening to yourself and being present. This time can be practiced in any number of ways, whether it is by meditation, yoga, prayer, daily walks, or just quiet time to reconnect with your own body and mind. For some people, it may only need to be as little as a few minutes a day, while for others, over an hour. There is no right or wrong, and it is up to each individual. I have found that if you spend this time in the same place and time each day, it is easier to become routine. To begin this process, change your voice mail to let people know that you are currently not available, turn off your phone, and embark on this personal journey.

A friend of mine, Julianna Raye, is a mindfulness coach. Her daily meditation routine includes anywhere from 15 minutes to an hour of formal sitting practice. She also goes on extended silent retreats where she practices up to 18 hours a day! This helps her be a better coach. She teaches people how to bring mindfulness meditation into their daily life, so your whole life can become a meditation. Her recommendation is to sit formally in meditation for a minimum of 10 minutes a day.

Julianna became involved in meditation while pursuing her passion as a professional singer/songwriter. According to Julianna, "It's beyond tough to break into the music business and I'm one of the lucky few who saw my dreams and aspirations come true, as overnight, I got a record deal on Warner Brothers, with iconic producer Jeff Lynne producing my music. It happened so quickly and easily I didn't have the perspective to consider just how lucky I was. That is, until I lost my record deal 2 years later and found myself waitressing again. Then I realized I might never get an opportunity of that magnitude again. I hated waitressing and deeply wanted to continue on my professional path of music and creativity. I did end up having more amazing professional opportunities in music over the years, but it's a hard road. Especially nowadays, the lifestyle can be grueling, even when you're very successful. So, sometimes you get to do what you're passionate about only to discover that you don't like the lifestyle that goes along with it. And sometimes you realize that there's a layer deeper. You discover an even more meaningful passion hidden beneath another passion. That's what happened to me. I'll explain what I mean."

Julianna continues, "When I was waitressing, it dawned on me that while I may have felt justifiably unfulfilled in my role as a waitress, I had also struggled to find fulfillment even when I was living my dream, making music and doing what I loved, full time. Music was so important to me, I was afraid the rug would be pulled out from under me. That made me relate to my career with doubt and fear, always feeling the pressure. I became preoccupied with holding on to my opportunities, which was an unhappy way to live. When things didn't work out the way I hoped, I was at risk, emotionally. I had struggled with severe anxiety and depression and when I went back to waitressing, I could see myself beginning to sink again.

That's when it hit me that opportunities were going to come and go, but if I wanted true and lasting happiness, I had to find it independent of the ups and downs of the crazy business I had chosen for myself. I had to find happiness or well-being that wasn't married to what I passionately loved to do. Because, as long as I linked those two inseparably, I was at risk if things didn't go my way. I had to become passionately engaged in everything I did, in order to free myself from the belief that passion could only come in a few specific forms. I had to learn how to make all of life a passionate journey, including the most mundane moments. I found a way to do that through mindfulness meditation and it freed me, profoundly."

Julianna said, "At a certain point, I discovered that mindfulness meditation was the deeper passion hidden below my passion for self-expression. Practicing mindfulness became the anchor at the center of my life. This happened naturally over time. It had started out as a way to heal myself emotionally. As I became stronger and happier over time, I had more and more energy to give to helping others learn the skills I had learned. Eventually I came to recognize that as much as I love the creative process of making music and performing, with all the training and experience I now have, empowering people with the skills of mindfulness feels like an even bigger gift to offer. I also saw that when I placed mindfulness at the center of my life, it made my creative expression more meaningful. It strengthened my music and performance. So, I didn't have to choose to do one or the other. Discovering this hidden passion of mindfulness below my original passion of music led me to rearrange my priorities, which has brought my whole life into alignment."

YOUR INNER CIRCLE

It is easy to become immersed and self-absorbed while exploring your passions. Be careful not to allow this to consume you, and maintain your relationships with family and friends, more importantly those in your inner circle. I am referring to the people you most want to be around because they care about you, support you, love you, and believe in you. Without an inner circle of family and friends, you will never truly gain fulfillment from your passions. Just as we never know how much time we have in our lives, we never know how long the people who are close to us will be with us. Throughout our lives, we go through different stages of appreciation, selfishness, and compassion. Although I speak about removing negative people from your inner circle, I want to clarify that I am not suggesting that you remove them from your lives entirely. People are each unique in their own way and even our closest friends and loved ones may not see eye to eye, or are driven apart by greed, misplaced anger, or simply having grown apart. People will have faults or beliefs and opinions that differ from our own. I am not immune to these situations and, as a result, have been able to identify negative influences in my inner circle throughout my life. Respect the diversity of all of the people who share this planet and do not judge others based on the criteria upon which we choose to live our own lives.

BE FEARLESS

The dictionary defines fear as, an unpleasant emotion caused by the belief that someone or something is dangerous, likely to cause pain, or a threat. The keyword in this definition is "belief". One of passion's greatest enemies is fear. Fear is not a quantitative measurement nor is it something tangible; rather it is strictly an emotion that we believe to be real. If we allow ourselves to, we can be paralyzed by fear. Living fearlessly allows opportunities for experiencing things far beyond your imagination.

I have learned to trust the systems in place for the things in which I have no control. In skydiving, for example, you learn how to position your body during free fall, learn how to pack a parachute, and intellectually you understand the entire process. Despite all that I knew, I still had to overcome my fear of jumping out of a perfectly good airplane. I needed to have confidence in my instructor, and trust that the equipment and all of the systems that were put in place would keep me safe. At 15,000 feet above the earth, I trusted the system, took my first step out of the plane, and experienced the exhilaration of falling at 120 mph. It was a huge adrenaline rush and my heart felt as if it was pounding out of my chest until my chute opened and I landed safely.

My good friend Todd Chroman has battled fear for much of his life. Todd explained, "For as long as I can remember, fear has always been a part of my life, living with it I mean. It is such a hindrance having to live in fear, never living life even close to its potential, and frankly, it's a waste of time and over rated. My greatest fear was flying. I had a mental block that was impossible to overcome. As much as I tried, I couldn't get onto a plane, and it took me over 20 years to let myself out of the cage I put myself in. Every time I would drive someone to the airport, I would think to myself, how do they do this? Why am I such a coward? How come I can't be like everyone else?"

Todd continues, "My fear started from childhood, which caused me not to trust myself, and prevented me from doing the things I really wanted to do. I guess my fears started at age 7, trying to deal with the murder of my dad, then shortly after dealing with an alcoholic and violent step dad who carried a gun, then growing up in a neighborhood where one had to learn how to defend oneself. I was terrified of schoolyards and confrontations with the bigger kids, as I looked like an older kid myself. As I grew older, I really wanted to see the world, but it was difficult having to drive everywhere."

Regarding Todd's battle with fear, he said, "I tried so hard to overcome my fear, driving myself to the airport and watching the planes overhead take off and land. Watching the people walk into the airport, walking through the open sliding doors, with baggage in hand, dreaming of the places they might be traveling to. One time, I purchased a ticket to fly 90 miles north of Chicago, and then waited at the gate, losing confidence by the second. Finally after sweating like crazy, I decided to try again another time and asked for a refund for my ticket.

Then one day, I just had enough weight on my shoulders and was watching something on *60 Minutes* about fear. The storyline was about a young girl who had fears and was taught to express them. This was missing in my plan, and I liked the idea. I started to say I could use this new idea to formulate a plan of attack. I looked in the mirror and started to tell the face in the mirror my greatest fears, over and over again. The plane will crash, the plane is going to crash, and repeated it for what seemed like hours. Then I finally cracked a smile to myself and felt better. I knew I had a chance to accomplish my dreams. Next, I volunteered to be the chaperone for my son's senior trip to Florida. I was honest about my chances of success, and gave myself a chance. Next, I discussed my situation with Carey and he suggested we drive to the airport and do a practice run. When we drove in front of those sliding doors, I dreamed of walking through, I asked Carey if he had any suggestions for me, and he told me to trust everyone from the baggage handlers, to the ticket counter people, to the flight attendants, as well as the pilots. Just surrender and trust, 100 percent. I then felt a little better about my chances. The last missing element was my little secret, just trust myself to walk through the airport, get to the gate calmly, and, if I could get to my seat and put my seatbelt on, I could handle the rest. It all happened the way I imagined. I made it to my seat and put my belt on, closed my eyes, and said to myself, 'I could totally do this'. After we landed in Florida, I was walking on clouds at how proud I was of myself."

Todd concludes, "From that moment to today, I have traveled the US and have enjoyed everywhere I have traveled to: Las Vegas, Los Angeles, Florida, Wyoming, Texas, Seattle, New York, Alaska, Mexico... Life is amazing. Best of all, I trust myself, the man I am and my decisions of traveling the world, with my beautiful wife, and knowing I can handle myself, and boy it feels great!"

The fight-or-flight response is a physiological reaction that occurs in response to a perceived harmful event, attack, or threat to survival, as first described by Walter Bradford Cannon. At this moment a person's reaction, to either save a loved one or prevent harm to them or themselves, is done without the cognitive awareness of fully processing the situation, thereby eliminating the opportunity of fear to play into the equation. If you live your life fearlessly, fully engaged, and fully aware, you are also better equipped to deal with negative situations should they arise.

Being fearless encompasses the understanding that you will inevitably make mistakes. Mistakes are part of the growth process of learning. When we limit ourselves, as a result of our fear of failure, we are not allowing ourselves to grow and experience new things. Attempting anything new can be scary at first, however, if you face your fears and do it anyway, you will grow from it and become fear-less. The dictionary defines "comfort zone" as, "a place or situation where one feels safe or at ease and without stress." Society wants us to be safe and to live in a comfort zone. We have all heard the say-ing, "NO PAIN, NO GAIN". I believe that pain is a crucial element in the road to success and you must step out of your own comfort zone to experience this. I suggest that you don't just step out of your comfort zone, but you LIVE outside of your comfort zone! Personal growth through the discomfort of real life experiences, will force you to grow, face your fears, and create your own success story. John A. Shedd said it best; "A ship in harbor is safe, but that is not what ships are made for."

4

DREAMS, GOALS & ACCOMPLISHMENTS

A dream can be perceived as a visual creation of the imagination. Without this vision, there is no direction, and without direction, there is no plan to get you to your destination. How many times have people made New Year's resolutions that were never kept? The gyms are filled with people working out after the new year, wanting to get into better shape. Eventually, with time, they begin to show up less and less. Not because they no longer want to be in better shape, but because they have not truly committed to it. Oftentimes, we speak of our dreams in the abstract, as if they are only pipe dreams, never to truly be realized. The first step in pursuing your dreams is to acknowledge them and therefore make them real. This can be accomplished simply by writing them down and listing your dreams for the next year, one to five years, and five to ten years. By documenting your dreams, you are creating a vision to determine what you truly want in life. By setting a time frame, you make it measurable, and can track progress along the way. Finally, when your dream becomes reality, you can celebrate your success. Once you have done this, you are on your way to making them come true.

Matthew Kelly, author of *The Dream Manager*, suggests making a list of one hundred dreams. I have had the privilege, over the years, to listen to Matthew speak at numerous conferences I have produced. Matthew stated, "When we know the dreams of the people around us, our natural response is to help them live those dreams."

While reviewing numerous note pages in writing this book, I came across my own dreams list that I had written about four and half years ago in one of my many digital note pages on my phone.

This was my dreams list:

1 Year

Expand my entertainment and production business globally
Take an adrenalin-filled trip with my son for his 21st birthday

1–5 Years

Take a cruise to Alaska with my wife
Open a west coast office in San Diego
Write my first book

5–10 Years

Have a second residence in San Diego
Write, record, and release a song

I had completely forgotten about this list and when reading it, I realized that everything on that list had been realized within each of the time frames I originally had set. Subconsciously, these were all things that I wanted to have happen and, even without the list at hand, they had come to fruition. As a matter of fact, my wife and I have already been discussing the feasibility of my ten-year dream. Acknowledging and sharing dreams is extremely powerful.

I recently came across a digital file from 2011, when my daughter Rachel wrote the following on one of her college entrance documents: "I have learned from my parents that anything is possible in life with dedication, perseverance and passion. I am passionate about helping others and excited about the prospect of teaching our future generations." I am proud to say that Rachel is now a special education teacher, fully pursuing her passion.

SNAPSHOTS IN TIME

Photographs capture a moment in time and allow us to revisit that moment by seeing the picture, which triggers our memory, and allows us to recall that particular moment or experience. If we could capture a particular accomplishment, or experience, in life, it would be like a snapshot in time, as it would tell our story of who we were at that very moment. The collection of these accomplishments, or experiences, helps paint a picture of us as a person, as it unfolds the story of our lives. My story is ever evolving because my passions continue to evolve. I am constantly in search of the next opportunity to experience as much as I can in life.

I have experienced major obstacles and setbacks throughout my life, as all of us do. However, I have never let these prevent me from pursuing my passions and dreams. The question is for all of us, "How bad do you want it?" If the struggle does not seem worthy of the reward, then there is no incentive to struggle. I feel that each struggle is an opportunity to grow and as a result I have had amazing snapshots in time throughout my adult life. I share these with you to prove that if I can overcome these life lessons, then anyone with perseverance can do so as well. I am proud of my achievements, but I do not rest on my laurels. We can always be more and do more with each passing day. I offer you my personal testimony to the capacity of what can be achieved throughout life.

Below are some snapshots of my incredible journey through life:
- Born into this world
- Became a Bar Mitzvah
- Lived in Israel for 6 weeks
- Hiked up Masada in Israel and witnessed a sunrise
- Won the first-ever title of Mr. United States 1984 (male version of the miss America pageant)
- Married to the love of my life for almost 28 years
- Proposed to Diane, bought our first home, and started living the American Dream at the age of 24
- Rappelled down waterfalls in Costa Rica

- Whitewater rafted on the Pacuare River on class 3 and 4 rapids
- Zip-lined over the canopy of a rainforest
- Saved someone's life from drowning (twice)
- Helped a friend overcome his fear of flying
- Had a pony tail for two years
- Swam with dolphins
- Contributed as an author to a bestselling college motivational book
- Played 9 characters in the theatre production of *The Dining Room*
- Acted in dozens of movie and television roles
- Have an amazing son, daughter, and son-in-law
- Took my son, when he was five years old, on a cross country trip to Lopez Island (off the Seattle coast) by plane, car, ferry and sea plane
- Traveled with family to Jamaica, Spain, Mexico, the Caribbean, continental U.S. and Alaska
- Took two father-son fishing trips to the Canadian wilderness
- Played chess with a U. S. Chess Master – many times
- Co-hosted, produced, and distributed a 30 minute video; "Everything you always wanted to know about cigars, but were afraid to ask"
- Past President (1993-1995) of International Special Events Society (ISES) Chicago Chapter

- Produced an international conference in a castle in Banff, Canada
- Became a P.A.D.I. Certified Scuba Diver, Advanced Diver, and Rescue Diver
- 2006 Cigar Champion Roller at the Chicago Big Smoke (La Gloria Cubana)
- Held my mother in my arms as she took her last breath
- Jumped out of a plane at 15,000 feet above Las Vegas
- Competed in Chicago's Urbanathlon (2008), Half Marathon (2009), Warrior Dash (2011), Metrodash (2011)
- Rappelled down 27 stories of the Wit Hotel in Chicago, three times for charity.
- Performed for over a million people since 1978
- President and Board Member of several nonprofit organizations
- Founding board member of Front Row Foundation
- Took three Front Row Recipients on experiences
- Recipient of the GALA AWARD for "Best Entertainment Concept" Awarded by Special Events Magazine (the Oscars of the Special Events Industry).
- Recipient of multiple NICE AWARDs for "Best Entertainment," "Best Use of Technology," and "Best ISES/NACE Team Event" Awarded by NACE ISES Chicago Excellence.

- Awarded 2011 "DJ of the Year" in the Reader's Choice Awards from BizBash Magazine.
- 2012 Recipient of the LIFETIME ACHIEVEMENT AWARD at the 13th Annual Entrepreneurial Excellence Awards.
- 2015 Recipient of the ISES Esprit Award for "Best Team Event"
- 2015 - Wrote, sang, recorded, and released six songs available on all digital stores worldwide, and three music videos.
- My wife and I created an amazing wedding for our daughter, and her husband

...and I'm just getting started!

"A man can be as great as he wants to be. If you believe in yourself and have the courage, the determination, the dedication, the competitive drive and if you are willing to sacrifice the little things in life and pay the price for the things that are worth"
—Vincent "Vince" Lombardi

THE PERFECT SONG

When my daughter became engaged, it was a surreal moment, as it would be for any proud father. Flashbacks of my baby girl growing up into the amazing woman she has become only reinforced how fast time had gone by. When it was time for me to create amazing entertainment for my daughter's wedding, this was not a problem, because that's what I do. I, however, also had the challenge of finding the perfect song for our father daughter dance. I wanted to dance with her to a song that fully expressed my deepest feelings for her and there was not a single song that I felt accomplished this daunting task. To me, the existing songs were either played out or didn't convey all of the raw emotions that I wanted to share with my baby girl. I came to the conclusion that the only way I would find the desired emotion and message in the perfect song, was to write, sing, and record my own pop ballad (which I had never done before). This would be the only way I could guarantee it being exactly what I wanted to share with my daughter, while also giving my daughter a very special gift from me. I would not only be sharing my creative talents and passion in the form of a song I created for her, but a song that she

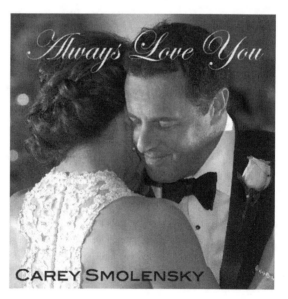

could cherish even after I am gone.

The process was an emotional roller coaster of which I can only describe as a labor of love. Between the tears, I created the lyrics and worked with my producer, Jay Dillen, to create the perfect melody that was both emotional and elegant, and also represented my beautiful daughter. This melody was created to fit my vocal range and when completed, I flew to California to record it. I created the song with personal references; however, these references are also generic enough for most fathers and daughters to relate to, and with which to identify.

My daughter shared eight magical words that made the journey of creating my song, "Always Love You" all worthwhile; Rachel said, "This was absolutely amazing Daddy - I love you!"

I am proud of my song and knowing that other fathers and daughters will listen to it, dance to it, and share in the raw emotions, is just an added bonus.

REBOOT

I have remained in business for almost four decades, not by looking at my competitors, but by focusing on our company's creativity, innovation, and continual evolution. When I started **Mobile Music Interactive Entertainment** in 1978, I introduced interactive concepts to the Chicago social scene. Our innovations included elaborate overhead truss lighting systems, holographic glasses distributed to guests to heighten their visual experience, a custom-designed light guitar that actually had built in technology to run our light show (while the operator was jamming on the guitar), and the first interactive dancers to hit the scene. We ruled the market. Eventually, other companies created similar formats, and then east coast companies entered the market, which only helped to increase demand as well as pricing. Through the years, most of our competitors have come and gone, while we still remain strong. It is the same in life as it is in business: you need passion. Without passion, work (and life itself) is not fulfilling.

Carey Smolensky Productions, the event production arm of my family of companies, has gone through many "reboots" over the past three decades. We support corporate conferences and summits, motivational speakers, multi-level marketing companies, and just about every industry imaginable. Recently, we combined our resources and skill sets in order to better serve our clients in the areas of edutainment, conference services, and explorative summits. This has not only allowed us to evolve in support of our clients' ever-changing needs, but continues to keep us an indispensable part of their team as we cultivate and maintain mutually beneficial relationships.

In 2007, I added my second entertainment brand: **STORM Interactive Entertainment**. This cutting-edge concept evolved out of my wanting to deliver something more than what we were already providing. We added live musicians, percussionists, vocalists, beatboxers, rappers, cirque performers, and new levels of special effects and video mapping technology. This division has grown tremendously (aside from being the entertainment at my own daughter's wedding) with a focus on targeting more of a national and global market.

As a result of having the passion to continually evolve, I have brought new life into each of my entertainment and production brands. Each "reboot" has not only allowed an increased level of enjoyment for both me, as well as my team, but for our clients as well. In addition to bringing on new clients and increasing bookings, our customer satisfaction is at an all-time high.

STAY THE COURSE

Whatever you do in life, keep dreaming and never allow life to pass you by. Get away from any bad habits that do not serve you well. Everyone has a story; use yours to empower yourself. The road to achieving your dreams is not an easy path, but it is well worth it. Along the journey, you will want to quit, because it is the easy thing to do. Don't succumb to quitting. Quitters never win and winners never quit! C.S. Lewis said it best: "Hardships often prepare ordinary people for an extraordinary destiny." With passion and perseverance, you can create your own extraordinary destiny.

5

THE 5-MINUTE RULE

Humans are naturally emotional creatures. It is important to understand the impact that our emotions can have upon our cognitive process in order to better understand whether or not we are in a proper frame of mind when making a decision or completing a task. This is because emotions are unpredictable, and are often considered irrational occurrences that come and go and may distort reasoning. We often see people react emotionally first and then rationally thereafter. Because of this, we should never attempt to solve a challenge analytically while being in a highly emotional state.

I have learned to not allow other people's negativity to infiltrate my psyche, affect my positive attitude, or sway me from my focused goal. I do not allow negative thoughts to remain with me; I replace them with positive thoughts. To put this in basic terms, a problem, or rather, a challenge is simply a situation that is in need of a solution. Rather than obsessing with a challenge that has already presented itself and cannot be undone, I choose to focus on finding a solution and moving forward. This process has proven invaluable to me numerous times in my professional career, and without the clear focus and determination, I would have not been able to find the correct solution.

One day, I was driving past an elementary school and noticed that the car behind me was tailgating me. The driver was visibly annoyed that I was driving so slowly, even though we were in a 20 mph school zone. When I came to a stop sign, the driver drove around me, blasted her horn, and sped past me. The driver missed her next light, and as I pulled up alongside the other car, I saw the driver hitting her steering wheel impatiently, while waiting for the light to change. The car kept inching towards the intersection, and when the light turned green, the driver peeled out, crossing over two lanes of traffic.

I don't know what the other driver may have been experiencing that day or what was happening at that time in her life. I do know, however, that driving, while in her highly emotional state, was not only a danger to herself, but also a danger to me, along with anyone else that may have been on the road.

Emotions can be influenced by any number of factors. Fear, anger, frustration, sorrow, and even euphoria, can each cloud one's judgment in any given situation. When something negative happens to you; when faced with a challenging situation, you have complete control to decide on how to respond.

If you are carrying anger, sadness, hatred, hurt or any negative emotion, then your decision of what to do next will be based on pure emotion and this will not be the clearest and most rational option.

By applying the 5-minute rule, we can detach our emotions from the actual situation so that we can make a more analytical decision. Practice and use the 5-minute rule in the following ways: If a bad thing happens, it's ok to be angry and process it, but for no more than 5 minutes. You can choose to realize that this is something that happened, it is in the past, and you cannot change it. So give yourself 5 minutes to deal with it. After 5 minutes, let it go! Clear your head, regain your composure, and focus on what you need to do to move forward to find the right solution.

This may seem easier than it is to do, and while that may be the case in the short term, with practice, it is not only possible, but it is an extremely effective tool in managing your ability to cope with the situation at hand. There is nothing more you can do about what was done, but you can choose to focus on where to go and choose which path to follow. I am not suggesting that this is a solution to the problem; what I am suggesting is that if you learn to let go of the things that are beyond your control, then you will be in a better mental state and will have a clearer mind to choose the next step you need to take in dealing with that situation.

A number of years ago, I was producing a national conference in Florida for my client, Vector Marketing. There are numerous components involved in producing this caliber of an event. Aspects include stage set, backdrop, video projection, sound support, video camera feeds, lighting, production, event management and all of the technology required to accomplish my client's goals. I arrived the day before setup with my crew scheduled to fly in the next morning. I do this for a number of different reasons, but part of this is a failsafe, because I always want to cover my back and be prepared for any eventuality.

At 10:00 that evening, I received a phone call informing me that the truck, with all of our gear, was just in a major accident. In the truck was specialized trussing, all of the components for a video wall, rigging equipment and motors, stage backdrop; everything for the conference and breakout sessions. There are a number of ways you can handle challenges and this was a true test to my own processes. I implemented my 5-minute rule, although I probably spent 10 minutes processing this one. I absorbed the situation and immediately started to figure out what I needed to do to not only make this conference happen, but to also deliver everything I promised to my client. To me, my word is my reputation and I do not take that lightly. It was not just about delivering what was on the contract; it was about upholding my client's trust and not letting them down. At this point, I was the only one who knew what had transpired. I then informed my team and began to reach out to my numerous vendor contacts that I had created over the years. By morning, equipment started to be delivered from at least six different suppliers. We started assembling aspects of the event as the equipment arrived.

By late morning, when my crew was scheduled to arrive, my client, Scott Gorrell, would normally see some progression of the setup. By this time, we would at least have the backdrop setup, or the start of screens being built. I pulled Scott aside and I said, "I need to let you know what is going on right now, but I also want you to know that your event will go on as scheduled and I will do whatever I need to do to make it happen." I then explained the whole situation to him.

Scott put his hand on my shoulder, looked at me, and said, "Carey, how are YOU doing?" I was blown away. Putting that in perspective, Scott was genuinely concerned about me. This speaks volumes about Scott's character and why Vector Marketing is not my typical client, but an integral part of my life for almost three decades.

At that point, I shared the plans that I had in place with Scott. I had equipment that would be arriving at all hours, and that I, along with my crew, would be working non-stop for the next 36 hours to make it happen. During that time, we even brought in additional gear, because we needed to devise, on site, a different way to suspend the video wall, since equipment specifications had now changed. Literally as the doors were opening for the attendees to come in, the final connections were being made and we not only made it happen, but it was a stellar conference, and an experience that I will never forget.

Each of us will experience challenges, or disappointments, throughout our lives. How we choose to address a challenge is what makes the difference between overcoming the challenge quickly, or accepting the situation as a part of our lives and reluctantly dealing with it. The choice is completely our own. When experiencing a setback, never look to blame something or someone else for it. Keep momentum going by continuing to move forward and focus on identifying the cause, and then finding a solution. People find it easy to blame others, but each of us needs to take responsibility for the cards we have been dealt, and make the most of them.

We have no control about what happens to us, but we can always be in control of how we react to any given situation. You may get a dent in your car or maybe your favorite restaurant is currently out of your favorite dish. These are not problems; these are situations wherein you have the ability to control how each affects you. You can change your perspective and be thankful that you have a car and were not injured when it was hit. You can be thankful that you have food to eat, although it was not your first choice on the menu. Sometimes, we all need to put our lives in perspective and truly identify the differences between our wants and our needs. We need to realize there are people in this world that are much less fortunate than us and they would do anything to have our "problems". This is why it is important to be mentally tough and learn how to change your perspective. I have learned over the years to not compare my own problems with those of others and to be thankful for the life I have.

REALITY

I have learned to respect the game of life. I call it a game because each of us can control our own path, challenges, and strategies, while being governed by the rules of the game. The "rules of the game" correlate to the laws of the land in which we live and these laws can often change during the course of the game. The other players are all of the people around us: our friends, relatives, business associates and even strangers. Add one's ethics, pride, and even greed into the mix and you have a pretty interesting game; a game that closely resembles the interaction of each of us in reality.

Reality, in my opinion, is based on perception. What people perceive is usually what they believe, and this is based on what they observe. We often feel that some days are better than others. Is this reality or our own perception? If we truly feel this way, then it becomes our own personal reality. All feelings are part of an evaluative system that determines whether what we perceive is beneficial or harmful to us. Each of us can experience a different, unique reality while being present in the same situation or experience. It is how one perceives a situation that determines what is garnered from that experience. It is also true that, subconsciously, people can hear things in a way that they want to hear them, because that may be an easier way for them to deal with that information.

As an example, for many of us who like ice cream (or frozen yogurt), even though we know what we like, oftentimes we want to try different flavors. We do this just to make sure that we are not missing out on a flavor that we might like even more than our favorite. But there is always that one flavor that we like best, and we keep coming back to it, regardless of how many other flavors we try. For me, this flavor is mint chocolate chip, and if given a choice of a second flavor, it would always be peanut butter. Peanut butter, however, would never be my first choice. The dilemma is that if you could only pick one flavor, out of the multitudes of flavors available, you would feel like you were missing out on all the other flavors, or at least I would. You never win! We always think we want what we don't have, but it's all in one's perception. Our perception is subjective and is not always supported by facts.

ATTITUDE

We cannot change our past, predict our future, or control how others act (or react) towards us. In other words, these are situations completely beyond our control. Charles R. Swindoll, author of the book *The Grace Awakening*, writes the following about attitude, "The longer I live, the more I realize the impact of attitude on life. Attitude is more important than the past, than education, money, circumstances, failures and successes and much more than what other people think, say or do." He continues, "I am convinced that life is 10 percent what happens to me and 90 percent how I react to it." While there are many things in life that we cannot change, we are in complete control of our attitudes. Attitude can be changed as needed in response to whatever we are confronted with. People use the expression, "tomorrow is another day," in response to something negative happening today. I say, why wait until tomorrow? I believe you can start anew in just 5 minutes and do it today, for we never know what tomorrow will bring.

PERSPECTIVE

I enjoy observing anyone who is truly gifted at his or her craft. This can be a flair bartender, cirque performer, trial lawyer, actor, carpenter, or musician. I have had an amazing experience attending an EDM (electronic dance music) concert in Miami at the ULTRA Music Festival along with over 100,000 people. I have also had another amazing experience sitting front row in an exclusive musical session with Yo-Yo Ma performing at The Chicago Symphony Orchestra in a private room for 150 people. Each of these experiences was phenomenal, albeit at completely opposite ends of the musical spectrum. The first performer was Joel Thomas Zimmerman, better known by his stage name Deadmau5 (pronounced "Deadmouse"), who is a progressive-house music producer and the other, the most adored cellist on earth, who has garnered 18 Grammy Awards. My passion for music allows me to truly appreciate an amazing performance, regardless of genre, location, or audience.

> "If you look the right way, you can see that the whole world is a garden."
>
> —Frances Hodgson Burnett, *The Secret Garden*

By changing your perspective to a positive outlook, you will naturally create positive change in your life. It will take some practice, but like anything in life that is worthwhile, once you have mastered viewing life's situations differently, the rewards are great. Here are a few perspective changing tips: Always focus on the solution, not the problem. Never allow negative thinking, or people, distract you from your goals. Change the way you think; anger and hatred are self-defeating.

Control the situation; don't let it control you. Be positive; it's attractive.

On a return trip to Chicago, after producing a conference in St. Louis, my flight was delayed at the gate. We eventually boarded the plane and were delayed again on the tarmac. We were then informed of a ground stop in Chicago due to weather conditions and eventually we returned to the gate and needed to deplane. I was anxiously checking the time because I was on my way to the premiere of a recent movie I had acted in, which was to be shown shortly after I was scheduled to land. As soon as I realized that there was no way I was going to make it in time, I used the 5-minute rule to deal with this situation. I could have been upset at missing the premiere, but there was nothing I could have done, so I texted the director letting him know I would not be at the premiere. I then focused my attention on writing this story in my book. I made use of the time I had and was productive, rather than brooding about waiting impatiently while accomplishing nothing. Life is like a GPS Route: There are many twists and turns, as well as unexpected detours. We need to always have the ability to adapt on a moment's notice in order to live a highly effective and productive life.

Whatever your final destination may be, or whatever goals you may have, enjoy the ride. Don't get caught up in how you are going to get there. If you get overwhelmed, spend 5-minutes on it and move on. Be present in the moment and live your life with passion.

In doing so, you will have no other choice than to love the life you have each and every day.

> "Whatever thought that activates a negative mood in your life, absolutely doesn't deserve a single moment in your mind."
>
> —Edmond Mbiaka

6

A LIFE OF PASSION

Before you can be passionate about anything in life, you must first appreciate life itself. Appreciation of what it means to be alive and to fully experience life by whatever means you have available. Life happens, and it is very easy to take for granted the series of experiences we know as simply being alive.

Passion, to me, is the fire needed to light one's soul. Feeling the power of what really excites you is truly an amazing experience, maybe even surreal. Living each day with passion not only provides the drive to accomplish your goals, but also affords comfort in knowing that we have the power to live the life of our dreams while appreciating the journey along the way.

Once, after producing an event in South Padre Island, Texas, I had time to relax and enjoy an amazing seafood buffet on the deck of a local restaurant. I was enjoying the warm, perfect breeze, as I gazed across the gulf. I realized that we, as humans, really don't need too much to be happy. I could easily live a simple life on an island in a minimalistic fashion. Happiness is found in moments of joyful experiences. These experiences are different for each of us, however, for me, they include time with my family, feeling the adrenaline rush of pushing myself to my limits, exploring the beauty of nature above ground, below the ocean's surface, and even in solitude.

I consider myself to be a fairly low maintenance person. Don't get me wrong; while I do enjoy the finer things in life, like anyone else would, I am truly as comfortable on a bus as I am in a limo, or eating street food at 2 am as I am dining in a gourmet restaurant. I go through life with no preconceived expectations, and this has served me well, as I am never disappointed. I can enjoy kicking back while hanging at a local dive bar just as easily as attending a gala reception. Although I do enjoy certain luxuries, I actually prefer the down to earth, grass roots style of living, where I can interact with people from all walks of life. The reality is that some of the meals I have shared with people that were living in the streets have been far more fulfilling and rewarding, than some shared with pretentious companions at gourmet restaurants.

As a rule, I try to support local establishments and avoid the national chain restaurants. I pride myself in my abilities of seeking out amazing local treasures wherever my travels take me. I will usually sit at the bar or am happy to share a table, as I make a habit of trying to never eat alone. You never know if the next person you meet could impact your life, or theirs, in a big way. Of course, if I am working, scheduling, or checking emails, this is not a very realistic option.

While in Dallas, waiting for my flight back to Chicago, I grabbed a seat in the airport bar. I was responding to an email, ordered a drink, hit send, and put my phone down. I looked up and glanced around the room only to see a multitude of people with their faces "glued" to their laptops, tablets, and phones; texting, playing games, and emailing, just as I had been doing only a few moments before. Even people that were traveling together sat in silence while each of them was on their own device, doing their own thing, immersed in their own world of virtual reality. I realized that most of us are addicted to our electronics and riddled with denial. Are we that afraid of being bored? Addictions hamper our judgment and prevent us from being present and in the moment. It is a fine line that we must balance in order to be productive, while not losing sight of being present in the moment we are in.

As I became increasingly aware of my surroundings, I overheard the conversation of some people sitting near me. A woman was excited about her new job and her new opportunities. As I continued to look around the bar and restaurant, I began to notice all of the people, from all walks of life, who were sharing this same space, at this particular moment in time, while waiting to go wherever they were going. I had been so wrapped up in my own world, my own business, and my own tasks that I, too, had failed to experience the moment that I was in. I noticed a song playing in the background.

The song had been playing all along, but until I was fully present in my environment, I was unaware of it playing.

What if your soul mate was sitting across from you, but you were each ignoring the moment by not being present? To live a life of passion, you must be fully engaged with your surroundings being present and in the moment at all times. A missed opportunity could be gone forever. What if a business opportunity could have arisen because other people were discussing a topic in which you could have contributed? When we shut ourselves out from the rest of the world with our ear-buds, or with our faces focused on our screens, we are not only isolating ourselves from others, but from all of the possibilities, opportunities, and potential experiences that could come to pass. I am guilty of this, on occasion, and constantly try to strike a balance between reality and virtual reality. As technology continues to develop, it becomes easier for us to communicate with each other, both faster and more efficiently. It also aids us in multitasking, however, in doing so, it takes away the human element and the personal experiences of interaction that life affords. Just a few minutes after I finished documenting this very experience on my phone and put it away, a gentleman sat next to me at the bar. We started a conversation that led to a potential business opportunity.

After having lived on this amazing planet for over half a century, and having started my family of companies almost four decades ago, I have interacted with people from all over the world and from all walks of life. I have learned to identify people for who they are, and not for whom I want them to be. In the words of C. JoyBell C., "Life is a bowl of cherries. Some cherries are rotten while others are good; it's your job to throw out the rotten ones and forget about them while you enjoy eating the ones that are good! There are two kinds of people: those who choose to throw out the good cherries and wallow in all the rotten ones, and those who choose to throw out all the rotten ones and savor all the good ones."

In the past, I had gotten into a habit of judging people's work ethic as compared to my own. I work as hard as I do because I strive to achieve excellence by the standards that I have set for myself. I have grown up working for everything I have ever owned. As a result, I became easily annoyed by the entitlement attitude I found in many people. This was not a very attractive quality and actually distracted me from focusing on my passions. I knew that I needed to adjust my own perspective, so as to not judge others by my own standards.

I have since learned to rise above any disappointments I see in others due to the high expectations I had set for them. I try to lead by example and avoid setting unrealistic goals for others. I have grown to understand that I can simply value the relationship for what it is, whether business or personal. In life we may perceive some people as being superficial, or even devious, but if we gave them a chance, they might just prove us wrong, and the relationship could blossom into a lifelong friendship or business alliance.

The more I experience in life, the less I am surprised by some of life's experiences. Although I have been affected by other people's actions, ethics or integrity throughout my life, overall, I am still a firm believer in the goodness of humanity. One bizarre example involved a past employee who actually lied about her brother passing away suddenly. She created an elaborate story of her feeling responsible for his death by her not being there for him, and as a result, she didn't show up to work for days, went completely off the grid, communicated like she was out of town and couldn't recall when her return flight was. This went on and on, compounding one lie on top of another, until the situation, and story, had escalated out of control. I felt sorry for this person, as she became so wrapped up in her web of lies that she felt there was no turning back and I never heard from her again.

There are people throughout my life that have taken advantage of my generosity or good nature and, although these experiences were extremely hurtful to me at the time, I have grown to become a stronger person as a result of each of these life lessons. I try not to harbor resentment or hold grudges because when a situation like this arises; it sheds light on exactly where I stand with these people, as they have shown me their character first hand. I can then determine if, and when, they have a place in my life, should I choose to continue any aspect of the relationship.

Family is the foundation of life and family members should be able to stick together no matter what. Unfortunately, sometimes greed, jealousy, tempers, illness, addictions, or egos can stand in the way regardless of how large or small the situation actually is. Communication is *always* the answer, and sometimes people may only hear one side of a story, make assumptions, or just don't take the time to listen.

"There comes a time in your life, when you walk away from all the drama and people who create it. You surround yourself with people who make you laugh, forget the bad, and focus on the good. So, love the people who treat you right. Think good thoughts for the ones who don't. Life is too short to be anything but happy. Falling down is a part of life, getting back up is living."

—José N. Harris

Each of us experiences life by whatever means we have available. Life just happens, and it is easy to take for granted all of the blessings that we have truly been given. There are many people who, for example, are disabled in some way, and do not have full use of all of their senses or abilities. What we may take for granted on a daily basis are precious dreams of those who lack those abilities. Usually when one sense is lost, others become heightened to help compensate. Each person, regardless of his or her personal state of awareness has, in my opinion, the distinct opportunity to truly appreciate life to their fullest extent. My son-in-law's mother, Suzy, is a perfect example of someone who appreciates life at every moment. After losing her vision just before her daughter was born, Suzy was determined to live her life with passion in every way she knows how. When interacting with Suzy, you would not immediately realize that she was blind. Her ability to adapt to her surroundings, combined with her confident demeanor and attentiveness to anyone addressing her is truly amazing. The more I get to know Suzy, the more passion for life I witness in everything that she does. In a recent conversation, Suzy shared with me that she was very fortunate to have been born with "an optimistic demeanor". Suzy said, "The cup is way past full for me. I attribute it to waking up happy each day and making it a good day." When I asked Suzy about her daily motivation, her reply was, "I want to always set a good example for my kids, who are now adults, each and every day. I think this is the underlying thing that drives me."

Each of us has the power to choose our own destiny regardless of our current situation. Suzy eloquently stated, "I choose to not let my blindness define me. I realize that I also represent disabled people, and I want to be a good example, and show others that we are a lot alike, and that I feel normal, too. Until I start talking about being blind." Suzy's perspective is not only inspiring, but is a true testament to her character. Suzy shared with me that she has found inspiration in other people, like Christopher Reeve, along with so many others who have a much tougher time than she does. Suzy concluded, "I am so lucky to have such a fantastic support system: my husband, my parents, and my kids. In this day and age, it is so possible to do anything... no excuses! I just want to be as "normal" as possible... but what is that anyway?"

Life provides us with an abundance of opportunities to appreciate beauty. Beauty is in the eye of the beholder – how true this really is! Whether someone is appreciating the operatic sounds of a singer on stage in the theater, or walking on a trail through a forest, or shredding a new coat of snow down a pristine mountain top, scuba diving below the ocean's surface, or gazing at the beauty of a field of flowers; each of these experiences will be beautiful to the behold-er, and all exhibit some of the many amazing things life provides. Whether it is an adventure, an experience, or an observation that is pleasing to us, each of us should truly appreciate beauty in its purest of forms.

I have always tried to share my values with my children and to teach them by example. Sometimes teaching comes organically, without any preconceived planning. For my son Blake's 21st birth-day, I wanted to do something memorable that would share my passion for living life to its fullest while providing us both with an adrenaline-packed trip that we would never forget.

Blake shared this experience in his own words:

"My dad took my cousin, Josh, and I to Costa Rica for a belated 21st birthday celebration. We went to Costa Rica in-stead of a 'typical' Vegas trip with the boys. My dad thought it would be a fun idea to do something adventurous instead of partying and gambling. Not to say we don't partake in that, but that's just the kind of person my dad is. He likes to do something memorable and different in every scenario.

On the second day of our week-long trip, we went white water rafting on the Pacuare River. On the journey to our drop off point, we were on a tour bus. The guide explains that we're about to enter the river at a class 4 (advanced) rap-id, and then it transitions into a class 3 (intermediate) rapid about half a mile in. Ok. Cool. I read the book *Downriver*, by

Will Hobbs, and I'm prepared mentally. We get off the bus and put our helmets and life vests on.

There were six people in our raft: the three of us, another couple, and our local guide. We hop in the raft, and start on down the river. We turn the first corner and there's a ten foot waterfall at a 45° angle. Half of us fell out: The girl from the couple, my dad, and me. The water is rushing all around, pinballing me off boulders and rocks underneath the surface. There's even a picture of my leg coming up out of the water. I finally got my head above water and grabbed the side of the boat. My dad had just surfaced as well. The tour guide reaches to pull him up, and he screams, 'NO! Get my son! Get my son!' They pulled me into the boat, and then we pulled him inside right after.

That's my dad.

While being tossed around underwater, I got a few, what I thought were, bumps and bruises. I hit my foot, my tailbone, and my neck. What I intuitively did was lace up my shoes tighter and kept quiet until the day was over. I found out a few weeks later that I had a bulging disc in my neck and I had broken a bone in my foot.

Looking back on this experience, I know I handled the pain the same way my dad would have. We were in Costa Rica on a trip of a lifetime! I couldn't let a little pain get in our way or slow us down. His needs were always secondary.

He would always sacrifice his own comfort to keep other people happy."

TIME

My parents taught me at a very early age not to waste time. While this may seem like a basic concept, the understanding of it is far more complex. It is very easy to lose sight of the important things in life. We are consumed by our busy schedules, routines, social commitments, never ending "to do" lists, emails, phone calls, texts, and a multitude of social media distractions. Each of these activities will take a toll on our time, and inevitably, our lives. Unless they are properly managed, we cannot escape from this rabbit hole. Let's look at this from a scheduling perspective; we should schedule time for us to enjoy our life, rather than just getting through each day. If we neglect to schedule time for ourselves, then our daily schedules become filled with other activities, meetings, projects, and even helping others. While each of these activities may feel important, unless we set aside time for ourselves and do this on a regular basis, it never happens and we can find ourselves asking, "Where did our time go?"

Every one of us has the same number of hours available each day. I will do more, sleep less, and outwork my competition all day long. Because once time has passed, there is nothing we can do to get it back. Use your time wisely and learn to be in control of time, rather than allowing it to control you. How often do we say, "I didn't have enough time," "I ran out of time," or "there are not enough hours in the day"? I believe that these are simply excuses that we have come to accept as explanations for our lack of completing a particular task. Humans are the only life form on earth that can choose to not live up to their own potential because of our freedom of choice. Use your freedom of choice to your own advantage. For example, I enjoy sports but do not choose to use my time to follow teams or watch most games. This is a choice that I have made from the realization that while I enjoy relaxing and watching a football game, I would much rather be participating in life first-hand, rather than experiencing life through watching the activities of others. This is only my perspective, and I choose to do things in life that challenge me physically, mentally and emotionally. Whatever I do to push myself, I always strive to inspire others.

The following lyrics are from the first song I wrote, "With Your PASSION":

> Time is something not easily grasped
> It goes and comes, yet no one asks,
> "Where did it go?" "Why did it leave?"
> You think it is abundant, you're the only one deceived
> Life is too short, so live it while you can
> Love is for the loving, love how much you can
> Motivate, articulate, demonstrate and never hate
> Front Row living right now, don't procrastinate

For as long as I can remember, I have always felt this way about time, life and love. I actually wrote some of these words decades ago, and they are still as poignant today in helping to convey my message.

Acting has always been one of my passions, but I had put it on hold while marriage, children, and business took precedent. In 2009, I decided to return to acting after a long hiatus. It is ironic that the first role I received was the lead character in a short film entitled, *Boycotting Time*, directed by Myles Hughes. The story is based on my character deciding that life is moving too fast for him, and he endeavors to boycott the very principle of time itself. I could not have selected a more suitable role for myself in which to resume my acting career. Life is truly stranger than fiction.

> "A man who dares to waste one hour of time has not discovered the value of life."
>
> —Charles Darwin, The Life & Letters of Charles Darwin

7

MORTALITY SUCKS

It is a trait of human nature, especially when we cannot overcome a problem, to attribute to it, some type of meaning. The ultimate problem for all of us is that inevitably, one day, our life will come to an end. The awareness of our own demise poses questions that delve into the very core of our existence. It is natural to search for some meaning in this, whether you turn to science, religion, or philosophy for answers, meaning, and comfort. The truth is that no one really knows for certain if there is life after death, the true meaning of life, or why we are here.

When faced with our own mortality, questions arise that reflect on the human condition as a whole. Aside from a religious perspective, it can appear that we are, as humans, living our lives in this universe much like a hamster in a wheel, or ants working and living in an ant farm. This simplified picture of humanity shows us that each person is born, lives their life, however long they have, gaining knowledge and experiences, and eventually dies. Of course, each of our experiences in life is unique, and as individuals, we cherish our family and relationships, sharing knowledge, and helping others. As a culture we honor our history and lineage. To me, death seems like an unfathomable waste of life, knowledge, and experience. The individual lives that are filled with brilliance and experience are inevitably doomed to be extinguished by death... scientifically speaking of course.

In an intellectual sense, we all know that life is short. But how many of us actually live our day-to-day lives as if we are really going to die one day? Many of us live lives filled with tedium, responsibilities, and unpleasant chores. We spend so much of our mental energy just getting through each day that it's easy to forget that our time on earth is finite. Any moment, however brief, if it is wasted, is time we can never recover.

Living each day with a heightened level of consciousness and awareness serves us well in preparing for the unexpected. It affords us the ability to respond to situations proactively, like in a game of chess. Allan Rufus, in *The Master's Sacred Knowledge* wrote, "Life is like a game of chess. To win you have to make a move. Knowing which move to make comes with in-sight and knowledge, and by learning the lessons that are accumulated along the way. We become each and every piece within the game called life!"

One of the many things I have learned from my Papa was how to play chess. He didn't just teach me how to play the game, he taught me how to think and strategize within the game. This has served me well over the years, as chess has since become one of my passions. I taught my son the game when he was just a boy, and, to this day, he has proven to be a worthy opponent. For those of you who do not play chess, it is a game of strategy and knowledge depicting a war between two kingdoms, using the board as the battlefield. Each player has sixteen chess pieces to use, and the ultimate goal is to win by placing the other player's king in checkmate. I have had the distinct privilege of playing numerous games of chess, on multiple occasions, with U. S. Chess Master Jude Acers in New Orleans, Louisiana. Jude is locally known for wearing a red beret and setting up his chess board by the gazebo in downtown New Orleans.

I can recall the first time I played Jude. His nonchalant, almost aloof, style is something to experience. He moved a chess piece and actually left the table, walked across the street to get a drink, and came back all the while I was still figuring out my next move. I held my own for a while and then began to see my demise. Jude made his next move and put me in a stalemate! For the non-chess players, this is a tie. In my opinion, it is actually more difficult to put your opponent into a stalemate rather than winning. By doing so, however, there is an understanding by both players of who actually won, it just is not flaunted. This was the work of a true gentleman. This impacted me so much that to this day, every time I play chess, I try to put my opponent in a stalemate. On my most recent trip to New Orleans, I asked Jude about his passion for chess. Jude said, "I feel strongly that passion affects longevity. If you have passion, it is usually for something that you want to live for."

I was in high school when my Papa passed away. I wrote the following poem, entitled "Life and Death" and dedicated it to him.

Life and Death

How can you describe a lifetime
A life of love and laughter
Of caring, wanting and experiences

How can you express a feeling
A feeling that you have
When the life you want to express it to is gone

Death is a funny thing
A scary, ugly, lonesome thing
But once it comes, you know it is too late

Life is for the living
Live it while you can
Love is for the loving
Love how much you can

If you love someone,
Let them know just how you feel
Let them know how much you really care
Before it is too late

CHOICES

I believe that we all have choices that can impact not only our chronological life, but the quality of our life as well. If you are not consistently learning, you are dying. Your brain "muscles", like any other true muscle, need to be exercised regularly and you need to always be challenging yourself.

I try to fill each day with as many experiences as possible. I have actually heard some people say that after 60 or 70 years, they will have had enough of life. I cannot even imagine that mind-set; similarly, I do not look forward to retirement as a goal. If I love what I do, why would I ever want to stop doing it? I want to keep evolving, learning, growing and setting new trends for others to follow. There is no limit to where we can go, what we can do, or what can be achieved at any age.

I was fortunate to have visited my friend Marty Domitrovich the week before he succumbed to cancer. As I entered his home, he was in a room to the right side, set up with a hospital bed. We reminisced about all of the events I had produced for him and Vector Marketing. Marty was a man filled with passion for life and perseverance. Marty would always end his presentations with a single spotlight on him, a vocal buildup with a music crescendo in the background, and at the right moment I would cut the music, and Marty would say, "What if Thomas Edison gave up?" We then cut the spotlight and as he stood in darkness, the roar of applause brought the lights back up. Marty was truly beloved by all who knew him. As we spoke, that day, it hurt me to see him in his condition and I was broken up. Marty, with a warm smile on his face, was more concerned with consoling me over how I was feeling, than for his own situation. Marty was a one of a kind person who truly lived life with passion.

LIFE IS PRECIOUS

While on our honeymoon in Hualtulco, Mexico, my wife and I were enjoying a beautiful sunny day while relaxing in the pool. I had noticed an elderly man standing in the deeper end of the pool, approximately 25 feet behind my wife, when suddenly I realized that the man was no longer there. Having been a lifeguard, while in high school, my instincts kicked in and I immediately began swimming towards where the man had been standing. There was a steep slope at the deep end and he had lost his footing. I saw the man at the bottom of the pool, unable to get to the surface. I took a deep breath and dove down to him. By the time I had brought the man up to the surface, there were other resort guests who realized what was going on, and had crowded around the pool. After surfacing with the man, I brought him to the side of the pool where other guests assisted me in lifting him out. After making sure the man was alright, I realized that during this situation, I had lost my wedding ring. When the other guests heard about this, everyone jumped into the pool until they found my ring. Looking back on this entire experience, I am fortunate to have been able to save this man's life. I am also fortunate to have been surrounded by so many people who were inspired by my actions that they chose to take action in order to do something to help me. Moments like these motivate me to always be present, cherish every second, and to be grateful for life itself.

One year, while vacationing with my wife and children in California, we were enjoying a day at Newport Beach. My wife and children were on the beach and I was body surfing in the ocean. I spotted a surfer nearby who was obviously in trouble, and I immediately swam towards him. The surfer was trying desperately to hang on to his board while in severe pain, experiencing cramping in his legs. Several times, I attempted approaching the surfer to assist him and bring him to shore. Each time I approached, he jumped on top of me in an effort to stay above water. I was comfortable with my lifeguard training and instinctively I pushed him away, dove back under, and came up again behind him. Although I had learned how to deal with a panicked victim in a pool, I was never faced with an actual situation like this, especially in the ocean and with heavy waves.

After repeated attempts to control the surfer by calming and assuring him that I was there to help, I eventually was able to reposition him in order to bring him back to shore, all while my wife and children were watching from the beach. My wife saw her husband in what looked like a desperate situation while simultaneously taking care of our four-year-old and six-year-old children. As I returned to shore with the surfer in tow, my body was not only covered with scrapes and scratches, but I realized that I had swallowed quite a bit of ocean water. When consuming seawater, the results of osmosis can be disastrous. Human cells have membranes which can prevent salt from freely entering our cells. The salinity of seawater is almost four times that of our bodily fluids. Although our bodies can tolerate salt to some extent, dealing with extremely high concentrations of salt in the blood is challenging. Unless you drink a lot of freshwater, the body's regulatory mechanism in this situation is potentially fatal. My body fluids were slightly depleted, my heart was racing, and I felt nauseated, experienced dry mouth and was, of course, extremely thirsty. It took several hours before I began to feel somewhat normal again.

I'm glad that I was in the right place at the right time, with the training that I had. You never know what circumstances life will put you in. You can, however, continue to learn new things throughout your life, because you never know when one of your life lessons will come in handy. I am grateful for this experience, not only because I was able to save someone's life, but despite the scratches, it has made me a stronger person, and reinforced my conviction to always help others and to do what is right.

WHY?

At some point in our lives, each of us will be faced with our own mortality. Whatever the cause, the result is an emotional experience that will be different for each person. The common thread is that, if we love and value our life, we do not want it to end. Being faced with mortality will not only change a person's perspective in an instant, but can lead to a traumatic and emotional chain of events that will impact an entire family, as well as their circle of friends.

Almost two decades ago, my wife, Diane, went to see her internist because she felt a lump in her breast. After the doctor examined my wife, he concluded that it was nothing and told her not to worry about it. He further indicated that, "At your young age, with a full plate, maybe you need to see a therapist." Diane's intuition told her that it was something more, so she immediately set up an appointment with a breast doctor.

The breast doctor initially wanted to do a needle biopsy, but Diane insisted that she wanted whatever was inside her removed. Whatever it was, it didn't belong there and she wanted it out. The doctor agreed to remove the lump, although he felt that it was un-necessary.

It was a Friday afternoon when Diane and I were at our office. Diane felt like there was a pit in her stomach, waiting for the biopsy results, which we were told would not come until Monday. Diane went home early and decided to call the doctor's office. The nurse answered and said, "Oh, the doctor wants to talk to you." At this point, Diane feared the worst and knew the news was not going to be good. The doctor got on the phone and indicated that although he originally thought it was going to be nothing, the pathology report came back and it was, in fact, cancer.

Diane recalled, "I remember collapsing to the floor screaming and crying and yelling, 'WHY?' I was in shock. I called Carey and said, 'you need to get home right away'. I remember immediately leaving our office, racing home, and running in the doors when Diane told me the news. Diane and I were now married for almost eight years and our son, Blake, was six years old and our daughter, Rachel, was four years old. Our perfect life had just been turned upside down. Diane remembered thinking, "After all that I had been through in my life, why was I being beaten down again? It didn't seem fair and I was angry and afraid. I knew that I had no other choice than to face this head on and fight."

After the surgery, the doctor told me, "Your wife saved her own life. She would have been gone in eight months." If the doctor had only done a needle biopsy, the cancer would not have been found, because it was located underneath the lump. If Diane had not found the lump in her breast and was not as persistent as she was, she would not be with us today.

The suggested protocol for treatment was radiation only, which would have provided an 85% survival rate after five years. This was not acceptable and Diane asked, "What else could I do?" The doctor said that chemo will increase the survival rate, but that Diane would be very sick and lose her hair. Diane said, "I don't care, sign me up."

After the initial shock, Diane was positive and became determined to beat cancer. Her treatments included chemo for four months, followed by radiation every day for six weeks. As soon as Diane's hair started to thin, she decided to shave her head, rather than letting it all fall out. She wanted to be in control and was determined to beat this. When our children came home that day, Diane told them that she was now like Steven. Steven was Rachel's friend, who, at the time, was also battling cancer and was bald. My mother-in-law took Diane to almost all of her chemo treatments and doctor appointments while I was at work. We never hid anything from our children, and tried to keep things as normal as possible for their sake. Diane never missed a day of work during her treatments and still participated in all of our children's activities with them. Our son, Blake, was old enough to realize his mother's battle and while some children might have been embarrassed about their mom being bald, Blake was proud of his mother and was always supportive of her. We bought an expensive wig, but Diane rarely wore it. She embraced her battle and was a true warrior.

Diane held my hand every night as we slept. She was afraid of what was happening and didn't want to leave me, or our children. There were birthdays, Bar and Bat Mitzvahs, graduations, weddings, and eventually, even grandchildren. There was so much more life to live and it was too soon to go. Diane recalled, "After learning I had cancer, I was working a Bar Mitzvah party and was crying in back of the room, thinking that I would never be at my own kids' celebrations."

Diane told me that if she died, she wanted me to re-marry, and that it would be alright for our kids to call my new wife, "mom", but as long as they remembered that she was their mom first. This is a true testament to Diane's character, and even though Diane is one of the strongest and most determined people I know, and was so determined to beat this, there was no guarantee of what would happen and she wanted to give me her permission.

As our children were growing up, we vacationed each year in Jamaica. Diane recalled, "I took a video at the ocean, thinking it might be the last time." As positive and determined as Diane was, there was still a side to Diane who thought that this might be her last trip. You never know and there are no guarantees. Diane described her perspective as, "We celebrated every school concert and every birthday as if it would be my last one. Every occasion became very emotional and still does. I wondered if I would be at our daughter's wedding and when I was, it was so emotional."

It has been said that you learn who your true friends are at weddings and funerals. We learned very quickly who our friends were as Diane began her battle. Many of our friends would bring dinners, call or stop by frequently, and support us emotionally, while some, even to this day, have completely disappeared from our lives.

I asked Diane to reflect on her mindset during her battle, especially whenever negative thoughts arose. I asked, "How did you remain positive?" Diane answered without hesitation, "I had to get up each morning and do what I had to do, to keep fighting."

THE BEGINNING OF THE END

One day, I was driving my mother to our home to stay with us while my father was recuperating from knee surgery. We were on the highway and my mom started to talk to me about her son, Carey. I will never forget that moment for as long as I live because that was the day I lost my mother. My mother had Alzheimer's, and that horrific disease gradually took her memories away over a period of sixteen years. My mother was a proud, strong woman who ran a business as well as the household. As the disease took away her most recent memories, her perception of time was only the period that she could remember. She soon would no longer know me, because those memories were gone and I was not born yet. She no longer would know my dad, because her time perception was now before they had met. When my father died, we could not tell her that he was gone.

My wife and I built an addition onto our home and moved my mother and her caregiver in to live with us for the remainder of her days.

My mother was no longer able to recognize herself in the mirror, because her memories were that of her as a young woman, and soon, with memories only of childhood, she relived the horrors of escaping from Nazi Germany. The last words my mother spoke were "please" and "thank you", because these are the first words we learn, and the last to be erased. My mother soon forgot how to eat and we were told it would only be a matter of time before my mom would stop drinking. I remember rushing home after events to spend every available minute with my mom.

What happened next was one of the most beautiful experiences I have ever had. My wife and I were with my mother when the woman who gave me life gasped to take her last breath. I was holding her in my arms and looking into her eyes when suddenly the haze of Alzheimer's was gone. I saw my mother and I felt that my mother not only recognized me, but it was as if her soul connected with me as she died. My parents were now both gone.

THE FINAL FRONTIER

When a person dies unexpectedly, it causes us to reflect on our own life and what is truly important. We look at how we spend our time and how we treat others. Tomorrow is never guaranteed and each day is a gift. This is why we need to make the most of our lives each and every day.

Leonard Nimoy, the actor who played Mr. Spock on *Star Trek* may be gone, but his final message on Twitter couldn't have been more profound. On February 22, 2015 the 83-year-old actor left the following bit of advice to his 1.1 million followers. After news broke of the actor's death, the tweet accumulated 47,000 retweets within an hour. The tweet was signed with the actor's usual tagline, LLAP – "Live long and prosper," echoing his iconic *Star Trek* character.

A life is like a garden. Perfect moments can be had, but not preserved, except in memory. LLAP

8

HELPING OTHERS

When on an airplane, we are instructed, in case of an emergency, to put on our own oxygen mask before helping others. This basic principle can be applied to every aspect of service in life. In order to optimally help others, you must be in optimal condition yourself. This concept is just as true for firefighters as it is for surgeons. Whether it is physical stamina and strength that is required, or mental clarity and precision, each of us must fine-tune the amazing machine we often abuse and neglect, known as our own body, in order to be able to function at our peak potential.

FUEL YOUR BODY LIKE A THOROUGHBRED

If you owned a thoroughbred horse, odds are that you would

only purchase the finest hay and grain to keep the horse healthy. That way the horse could race at its optimal performance level. A car requires gasoline to run, and there are a variety of gasoline choices to use depending on the desired performance of your car. In this same manner, your body requires fuel for energy, and just as there are different grades of gasoline, there are different types of foods to fuel your body. The timing, type, combination, and consistency of foods you eat each have an impact on your energy levels and performance. You would never think of feeding your thoroughbred horse fast food and chemicals, however, most people think nothing of ingesting fast food and preservatives into their own bodies on a regular basis.

It is important to fuel your body with nutritious food, stay hydrated, and get enough sleep. While this may seem obvious and simple to do, many of us do quite the opposite. With all of the responsibilities as well as distractions we have in life, many times, the decisions we make are based on convenience, rather than a plan.

It has been said that, "It is far better to give than to receive." While this may seem to be only a saying, it is a truth that speaks volumes and can only be fully appreciated and understood by someone who has authentically given to others without expecting anything in return. I share with you the following story, as it is not only poignant but speaks directly to the essence of this concept:

> Once upon a time, there was an old man who used to go to the ocean to do his writing. He had a habit of walking on

the beach every morning before he began his work. Early one morning, he was walking along the shore after a big storm had passed and found the vast beach littered with starfish as far as the eye could see, stretching in both directions.

Off in the distance, the old man noticed a small boy approaching. As the boy walked, he paused every so often and, as he grew closer, the man could see that he was occasionally bending down to pick up an object and throw it into the sea. The boy came closer still and the man called out, "Good morning! May I ask what it is that you are doing?"

The young boy paused, looked up, and replied, "Throwing starfish into the ocean. The tide has washed them up onto the beach and they can't return to the sea by themselves. When the sun gets high, they will die, unless I throw them back into the water."

The old man replied, "But there must be tens of thousands of starfish on this beach. I'm afraid you won't really be able to make much of a difference."

The boy bent down, picked up yet another starfish, and threw it as far as he could into the ocean. Then he turned, smiled and said, "It made a difference to that one!"

—Adapted from *The Star Thrower*, by Loren Eiseley (1907-1977)

There are so many amazing people doing amazing things, along with a plethora of noble causes available to support. When you truly give of yourself, without expecting anything in return, you experience giving in its most pure form. We are all the same, regardless of our personal beliefs, nationality, religion, color, sexual preference, or creed. The true beauty of helping another human being is beyond description and can be felt with an outpouring of emotions and appreciation for the beauty of life itself. I will highlight a few examples in order to demonstrate the diversity of not only the causes, but in the ways each of us can make a difference in the lives of others for the short time we are alive on this planet.

We are each busy with our own lives and often think, "What kind of difference can only one person make?" The truth is that every person has the power to make a difference and create positive change. Positive change is always worth making, regardless of how small we believe the impact to be. Every little bit helps, and, just like the boy throwing the starfish back into the ocean, each of us can make a difference in the lives of a few. With the help of other like-minded people, we can make a difference in the lives of many, and by taking massive action we can create a movement to impact the world.

It is easy to become consumed with the enormity of a situation and, as a result, become pessimistic, or, even worse, complacent to it. If we could only look through the eyes of a child, where nothing is impossible, we would be on track to a solution to any and every challenge we face. One person *can* truly make a difference. It takes courage, determination, perseverance, and passion, but the results will be worth the struggle. Be the beacon of light for others and teach through leading by example. If we humanize a problem as a challenge that people have, we can search for solutions.

HELPING IN A TIME OF NEED

A longtime friend of mine, Teddie Kossof, is the founder and owner of Teddie Kossof Salon and Spa, a high-end hair salon and spa located in Chicago's prestigious North Shore. A number of years ago, one of Teddie's client's sons, Jason, a high school football player, had gotten into a car accident at the end of his sophomore year. While driving, Jason got cut off and flipped his jeep. It landed on top of him and pinned him to the ground. Jason ended up paralyzed from his mid-back down.

Teddie explained, "On a Friday afternoon at the salon, Jason's mother approached me at the salon. She came in a month and a half after the accident, in a desperate state, and explained what had happened. She opened up to me and shared their financial situation. They had retooled their house to equip it for wheelchair accessibility and had to take out a second mortgage. She shared how hard it was logistically for her and her husband to both work while trying to get Jason to school, as well as her concern for her son's mental state."

Teddie came up with the idea of wanting Jason to become independent, and take himself to school. Teddie suggested doing a fundraiser to get her son a wheelchair-equipped van. Jason's mother started to cry and thought that would be amazing.

Teddie continued, "I reached out and went from business to business, I set up a chart in the salon, and asked the community for help. My clients donated, and one individual even contributed $5,000! Slowly we reached our goal of over $40,000. I was very emotional after working so hard to make this happen. I was so happy to go to the Ford dealership and purchase the van for the family. The van was specially equipped with hand controls so that in his Junior and Senior years, Jason was able to drive himself to school. Having been a football player, he became involved in wheelchair basketball, and had regained his independence. I am so proud to have helped make a difference in his life."

I asked Teddie to reflect on the community reaction to his fundraiser. He said, "Some people were very receptive and donated $5 - $25, while some were very cold to the idea of even donating. I learned a lot through this process, and a lot about the character of different people in the community. This experience helped me grow and I also gained a great deal of respect from the community that knew I was doing this all along."

IMPACTING LIVES WITH COFFEE

Throughout my travels in producing events and entertaining, I have had the honor of getting to know amazing people all over the world. One such person is Brendon Maxwell, the co-founder of Utopian Coffee Company. Brendon shared with me the story of his journey to living his life filled with passion, and it began 1,000' above ground:

"Sailing through the air, 1,000 feet ascended, I had to figure out a way to continue this. The view of the Remarkables mountain range on the south island of New Zealand was... well, remarkable. With my feet dangling in the air and my adventure throttle fully engaged, it was inevitable that I would continue traveling internationally, as much as possible, and to as many different places as I could point to on the vintage globe in my den."

Brendon continued to elaborate, "While this started out as a way to find adventure, learn about diverse cultures, and seek the unknown, it was setting the stage for what would be the foundation of my life's work and purpose. This desire, along with some entrepreneurial background, led me to co-found Utopian Coffee Co. with my cousin in the fall of 2006. With only $750 as our starting capital, there wasn't much (read: any) room in the budget for travel, but our desire was to connect my passion and love of international exploration with my cousin's industry experience and love of coffee and to tell stories that help better explain this product that is grown almost exclusively in the under-developed world."

What began as a vision by two young friends talking on a couch after dinner has manifested into traveling to micro lot coffee farms in remote areas throughout the world to build relationships, invest in people, and tell their stories that are often unknown and unappreciated. Brendon went on to reflect on his latest journey: "I just recently returned from a couple of weeks exploring in East Africa. Traveling through the Democratic Republic of the Congo and Rwanda, I was humbled by the incredible resourcefulness of people and by their work ethic that leads to the product we consume on a daily basis. As I sat in the painted green and yellow cinder-block restaurant, I was fortunate enough to hear the story of 61-yr-old Corette Nakabonye, who is the President of the female-owned and operated coffee co-operative from which we purchase. I got to listen to her, through a translator, talk about how she had been involved in coffee from childhood, as her father was a coffee farmer. Her tales of hard work and time investment over the course of decades was inspiring. And her heart and compassion for the women who are part of the co-op was contagious, as she yearned to find and create new opportunities that could bring economic stability to these partners of hers. Sitting there, surrounded by people who had endured genocide and were part of the re-birth of their country, there were no words that I had to express... just a feeling of gratitude. Grateful that I get the chance to be a small part of these people's lives and that I get to share these stories with our customers and supporters; grateful that I get to be welcomed into the narrative that is their lives; grateful that I get to be challenged and inspired to do more."

Brendon reflected, "It's not always easy to pursue what it is you are passionate about and that is one of the misunderstood fantasies. In Latin, *passion* was used in reference to suffering. And in many ways, that is a more realistic and accurate portrayal of what we're willing to endure in the pursuit of this mystery we refer to as passion. Whether its 26-hour plane rides, stomach illnesses that last for days or weeks, paying bribes, facing malaria, or any of the other accompanying challenges, I choose to suffer for these pursuits. But I can't imagine it any other way."

WARM CLOTHING & GIVING HEARTS

The United Nations Food and Agriculture Organization estimates that about 805 million people of the 7.3 billion people in the world, or one in nine, were suffering from chronic undernourishment in 2012-2014. There is poverty all around us and in this day and age, nobody on this earth should have to go to bed hungry. Clean water is a luxury in some parts of this world and we can all make a difference if we just did *something*. Whether in your own neighborhood, or another part of the world, be proactive and, in the words of Maya Angelou, "Be the change for the world to see."

One day, my wife and I were driving back home from Chicago with our two young children. We decided to use this opportunity to show them that there are people who were not only less fortunate than us, but homeless and living in the streets. We drove through Lower Wacker Drive, where many people were living in boxes and tents made out of worn sheets. This experience had a profound impact on our children, and they wanted to do something to help these people. We decided to make a difference, and our family, along with some close friends, got together and made sandwiches, collected clothing and had all of the children decorate lunch bags with drawings and personal notes. We got up early the next morning and drove, in caravan, through the areas where there were people in need and distributed bags of food, fruit, bottles of water and warm clothing to those we could help. Most importantly, we showed each person respect and made sure they knew that we cared about them and that they were loved.

Some friends of ours who had owned a restaurant in Chicago for many years would open their doors on Thanksgiving to feed the homeless. Our family had the privilege to be part of this amazing experience. We would serve up turkey, stuffing and all the trimmings.

We would wait on these people and treat them as our VIP guests. Aside from providing food, we provided them with a hug, a smile and most importantly, respect. Too often, people ignore the homeless and walk by as if they don't exist. This is a tragic element in our society, and there are many people that are one or two mortgage payments away from being homeless themselves.

In 2014, my company, Carey Smolensky Productions, started an annual "Warm Clothing Giving Hearts" drive. Our clients and vendors team up with us each year to collect warm clothing based on the example, originally set by our children, Rachel and Blake, years ago. We search out where many of the homeless live in Chicago and bring them clothing, food, water, and supplies. We spend time with them to make sure they know they are loved and respected. I will never forget a homeless man who cried when I shook his hand and hugged him. He told me, "Most people ignore me and treat me like I have a disease, like I'm not even human... and you touched me." Another man, who was living in a makeshift cardboard box beneath rags and towels, eventually stuck his head out to accept our gifts, only after much assurance that we meant him no harm. While so many of these stories are heartbreaking, they are on the other hand, a testament to human resilience and a desire to survive. In each area where they lived, there was always someone watching out for their group. It was as if they had a society of their own. It was inspiring to see, on many occasions, as we came upon a group to offer our help, that there were already bags of food, bottles of water and supplies already left by other caring individuals.

A DOCTOR'S PASSION

My daughter Rachel recently married an amazing man, Joe Falender. Joe treats my daughter as every father would want his own daughter to be treated. What I have come to learn is that Joe's family is just as amazing as he is and that Joe's father has a story that deserves to be shared.

Joe reminisced that, for the longest time, he could remember his father's screen saver that said, "Only you can control your own destiny." According to Joe, "Things that my father taught me growing up instilled in me not to be afraid of hard work, and the way he has gone about caring for my mother, after she became blind, speaks volumes about the type of man he is." Joe continued, "No matter what life throws at you, you have to be prepared to face its challenges, and no challenge is too hard to overcome." My dad has never treated my hearing loss (which I have had since birth) or my mother's blindness as a hindrance to living an amazing life with passion. Whenever going on vacation, regardless of the most mundane side trips, my father would say, "We are going to have an adventure of a lifetime."

Joe continued, "My dad has a job that allows him to help people every day, doing something that he is not only passionate about, but that also affords him gratification. In turn, he has taught me that there are no shortcuts in life, and to be passionate about what I love, and become the man and son that my dad always knew I would be."

In Dr. Lawrence Falender's own words...

"As long as I can remember, I wanted to be a doctor, and, more specifically, a surgeon. Of course, as a boy, I had the same aspirations as my friends: cowboy, astronaut or a John Wayne hero. When I was 13, a TV show, *Medical Center*, debuted and I continued to watch it for its 7-year run. It featured Dr. Joe Gannon, a surgeon, showing care, compassion, and great surgical skills in the operating room each week. I was mesmerized; that is what I wanted to do. A few years later, the TV show, *M*A*S*H*, cemented my desire. I wanted to be a surgeon with a great sense of humor like Hawkeye Pierce!!

My future wife, who was planning on a career as a dental hygienist, suggested I look into dental school. Additionally, a local oral surgeon allowed me to shadow him in the operating room during a jaw repositioning surgery. After graduating from the Indiana University School of Dentistry, I was accepted to an oral and maxillofacial surgery residency at Lincoln Medical Center in the Bronx, NY where I learned to always DO THE RIGHT THING! I have followed this mantra ever since!

One area of dentistry that intrigued me was caring for those patients who lost all of their teeth. In 1985, I was fortunate to go to a seminar by a Swedish surgeon lecturing on dental implants; titanium root replacements that allowed dentures to be secured even with limited jawbone. I saw the infinite opportunity for patients and was instrumental in establishing dental implants in my residency program and placed my first dental implants in 1986.

I eventually started my own oral surgery practice. Even though dental implants were not prominent in any local oral surgery offices, I was dedicated to offering this life-changing procedure to my patients. As an oral surgeon, I would place the dental implant into the bone, and then the patient's general dentist would fabricate the attached crown, bridge or denture. The problem was that the local dentists had no implant training and the dental school did not offer any for many years! I took courses on how to restore the dental implants and started the first dental implant study club in Indianapolis. This allowed me to teach general dentists how to do their portion. I also lectured to other doctors throughout the Midwest.

Within the past four years, I have added the All-on-4 treatment protocol to my practice as the first dental surgeon in the Indianapolis area to offer this outstanding procedure. This allows a patient to have a fixed, permanent replacement for their missing or soon-to-be-removed teeth. Imagine being told you need all your teeth removed, or you have multiple crowns or bridges that fail. I have been able to help so many patients with this TLC procedure: Truly Life Changing!!

This year, I decided to give back to the community. Along with general dentist Dr. Bryan Sigg, Larry Sowinski, and my staff, we picked a member of our community and performed the All-on-4 procedure without any cost to him. The recipient was a retired marine and current sheriff's deputy. His teeth were in need of removal. He did not smile and, it is worth mentioning that, as a police officer, a smile can diffuse many situations. In one appointment, I removed all of his teeth and placed dental implants in a specific position and angulation. Along with the dental lab owner, we converted prefabricated dentures into a fixed prosthesis and then secured into the implants. Imagine coming into the office at 8 am with a mouthful of defective teeth and leaving 7 hours later with a secure, beautiful smile. After four months, this temporary replacement will be converted into an attractive final prosthesis that will look and feel like natural teeth.

Being able to replace a missing body part (tooth) or a full mouth of teeth *and* have it look natural is a blessing. So, you ask, what is my passion? That's it: giving patients back their own missing teeth, restoring their smile and, as importantly, reestablishing their self-confidence.

This is why I have gotten up every workday and gone to my office for 27 years: a chance to help a patient. From the patient being in pain and needing a tooth removal, or the patient with an oral lesion who is worried it is oral cancer, to a teenager having his wisdom teeth removed, almost everyone is nervous.

I am passionate about the part I play in helping to change people's lives. Treating every patient as if they were my good friend or family; this is how I have practiced oral and maxillofacial surgery all these years and will continue to do so for years to come."

FRONT ROW FOUNDATION

In 2005, a small group of amazing people got together in Myrtle Beach to exchange ideas, collaborate, and brainstorm ways to make a difference in each other's lives and in the lives of others. This group of people wanted to make a difference in this world. I am proud to say that I was one of those people and our collaboration was the birth of Front Row Foundation. We sponsor recipients who are battling life-threatening illnesses by bringing them to the live event of their dreams in the "Front Row".

In the first decade of Front Row's existence, in addition to being a Founding Board Member and producer of the organization's fundraising galas and events, I have had the distinct honor of taking three recipients on their own Front Row Experiences: Michelle, RockStar Mike, and Kadeen.

MICHELLE (Age: 13)

Illness/Critical Health Challenge: Rare genetic disorder: Familial Dysautonomia

Event: WICKED, The Musical (Chicago) - October 14, 2008

The day began as Michelle, her nine-year-old sister, and her parents, were surprised at their home by a black stretch limousine that transported them to Wildfire Steaks, Chops & Seafood for lunch, hosted by the restaurant. The entourage was then whisked to the

Oriental theater, where they took part in the "Behind the Emerald Curtain Tour," followed by complimentary pre-show refreshments hosted by Argo Tea Café. The magic continued back at the theater, where the family was pampered with VIP suite service before enjoying the performance of *WICKED* in the front row. There was one last surprise in store: an exclusive meet-and-greet with the principal actors from the company, taking photos with them, visiting their dressing rooms and even trying on some of their costumes.

"The evening was unbelievable: it was beyond anything we could have imagined," said Michelle's mom. "It was magical...the people from the cast were fantastic, just so giving, and we were so surprised that all four leads came out to meet Michelle. The day was wonderful, not just for Michelle, but for the entire family. I was left speechless, and I know Michelle will always be thankful for such an awesome experience."

The look of amazement on Michelle's face was priceless as she experienced the magic of WICKED only 10 feet from the stage. For one incredible day, we were able to ease the pain and struggle of her illness and just let her be a normal teenager. That's why I am proud to be part of the Front Row Foundation: for the chance to grant someone's dream of seeing live theater, but in the front row so that they are practically part of the performance. To experience that kind of thrill through the eyes of such a special individual was truly amazing!

"ROCKSTAR" MIKE (Age: 19)

Illness/Critical Health Challenge: Tracheomalacia, an enlarged heart, pulmonary-hypertension, developmental delays, asthma, cirrhosis of the liver, enlarged spleen, and serious platelet issues.

Event: Pirate's Voyage (Myrtle Beach) - September 26, 2012

"ROCKSTAR" Mike's infatuation with pirates began when he was a young boy. He knew every "Pirates of the Caribbean" movie word for word, and he loved everything about pirates. When he was a little boy, he would protest brushing his teeth, saying, "Mom, pirates don't brush their teeth!" She finally convinced him – what a funny memory! Mike's Front Row Experience was filled with firsts: his first plane ride, first time seeing the ocean, first limo ride, and his first time seeing a pirate show.

Upon arrival at the Pirate's Voyage venue in his private SUV limo, Mike was greeted by pirates, who helped him out of the limo. He was a little frightened at first, but then settled right in to the VIP treatment. Dinner was served while watching the show, which Mike was excited about, because he didn't want to miss one moment of the show. The meal was "fit for pirates" including things like "buccaneer biscuits", "mashed & flogged taters", and "apple o'me eye pie". The food just kept coming, and Mike gobbled it all up! Mike sat back and took it all in: the silly acrobats, the loud captain, and the "real" pirates.

Shortly after "ROCKSTAR" Mike returned home, his condition deteriorated and he was required to sleep in an adjustable hospital bed placed in the family's living room. I visited Mike, along

with my wife, Diane, and son, Blake. Shortly thereafter, Mike was moved to a hospice facility. Right next to his bed was the Front Row Experience photo album that he would look at and remember his pirate's adventure.

"ROCKSTAR" Mike passed away nine months after his Front Row Experience at the age of twenty.

KADEEN (Age: 6)
Illness/Critical Health Challenge: *Juvenile Pilocytic Astrocytoma (brain cancer)*
Event: *Disney on Ice with Mickey Mouse (Chicago) - February 1, 2014*

On the cold, wintry day of Kadeen's Front Row Experience, a luxurious stretch limo pulled in his driveway to chauffeur Kadeen, his parents, and his three siblings to downtown Chicago. They arrived in style at The Ritz-Carlton for their getaway weekend.

Disney on Ice and Mickey Mouse could not have come fast enough for this super fan! We grabbed some sugary snacks, took photos, and made our way down to the ice to our front row seats! Within minutes, the ice came to life with real-life, skating Disney characters. At the end of the show, something magical happened! Pluto skated over to Kadeen, knelt down on the edge of the ice rink, and motioned for Kadeen to come closer. Then, Mickey skated up, then Minnie! They all motioned for Kadeen to walk over to them. Gingerly, Kadeen and his brother stepped towards the three characters and exchanged

handshakes and high-fives, before the characters skated off again. Kadeen was star-struck!! After the show, Kadeen and his family had a steak dinner (his favorite) at Joe's Seafood, Prime Steak & Stone Crab and a quick trip to The Disney Store on the Magnificent Mile. Kadeen slept the entire limo ride home, and talked about his Front Row Experience for weeks following.

REFLECTIONS

I asked my friend and Front Row Foundation co-founder, Jon Vroman, to reflect on the past decade of recipient experiences. Jon said, "We initially started doing this for the recipient, but soon realized the extended impact that was created. By helping the recipient, it supported their family and the community as well. We realized the ripple effect." We discussed what separates Front Row from the other wish-granting organizations. Jon pointed out, "It's not just about seeing an event and making a dream come true. It's about a lifestyle, a way to think about life, regardless of how many days we have." The charity is doing something radically different and is serving the global community in unique ways. The podcast *Front Row Factor* is hosted by Jon Vroman and provides information to help people maximize and appreciate their life through personal growth, powerful relationships, and making a difference. People have moved from the back row to the front row of their lives. Proximity is power and Front Row demonstrates how to live life as a participant, not a spectator. This is why Front Row is different. We are truly living life in the front row!

I asked Jon to share his vision for the future regarding the organization. Jon replied, "One day every live event around the globe would have seats reserved for Front Row Foundation." As the "head usher" of the charity, Jon will continue bringing people to the front row.

A YEAR TRAVELED

It is December 8, 2015, exactly one year to the date from when I first embarked on my journey to write this book. I am completing this final chapter on the very same flight back to Chicago that I took when I began my story. Having just produced the 2015 "Best Year Ever BLUEPRINT" in San Diego, this year it was partnered with the 10th anniversary celebration of Front Row Foundation. I am so proud to share that, at this single event, we raised over $110,000 for Front Row Foundation! Because of this tremendous success, we will be able to exponentially increase the number of future experiences for Front Row recipients. Moving forward, both of these events will continue to coincide with each other, mutually support each other, and continue to impact the people around us, and the world in which we live.

MY TRUTHS

The dictionary defines legacy as an amount of money or property left to someone in a will. To me, a legacy is more about sharing what you have learned, not what you have earned, and bequeathing values over valuables.

My wish for you is to follow your dreams, to live your life with passion, and to help others along the way. This magical journey through life is truly inspirational, beautiful, and profound.

I believe it is important to reflect on who you are, and what you stand for, and when you come upon a situation that tests your character, you can reflect upon it and remember what you are here for.

"Love your life, live it with passion, strive for excellence, and always help others."
—Carey Smolensky

POSTSCRIPT

A review of this book would be greatly appreciated. Please post your review on Amazon or spread the word to help inspire others. Thank you!

It is my wish that you live a life filled with passion and experience all that you desire. Always help others so that we can impact our world.

Much Love,
Carey Smolensky
www.CareysPassion.com

CONNECT WITH CAREY'S PASSION

FACEBOOK

Carey's Passion

TWITTER

@careyspassion

INSTAGRAM

@careyspassion

WEBSITE

www.CareysPassion.com

Made in the USA
San Bernardino, CA
21 December 2015